"Simon recounts his ~~~~~~~~~~~~~~~~~~~~~~~~~~~~~~~~oulin ~~uge in Paris and how it led t~~~~~~~~~~~~~~ywood in this debut book. Paris in 1988 wa~~ ~~ace of great beauty and great grit, filled with tantalizing women, bacchanals, street thugs, and enterprising criminals. Simon had the opportunity to rise from a replacement background dancer to a principal performer, a position that would prepare him for the even more competitive world of Hollywood. A colorful and illuminating memoir of a cabaret performer."
Kirkus Reviews

"*Paris Nights* is a memoir of how the author, Cliff Simon, managed his life in the Paris Theater after having lived in South Africa for a substantial time. He holds a loving regard for both Africa and Paris, expounding on the various riches of both lands. This view adds the kind of punch and freshness to a story that motivates the reader to turn pages. Discover a little French truncate along the way. Here is a guy who found love in recalling that part of French culture that sticks to your guts. Let's have a grand round of applause for Cliff Simon."
Manhattan Book Review – Star Rating: 4 / 5

"If the aim of a good memoir is to let the reader into someone's life and give them a taste of some interesting and unique experiences, then this book definitely measures up. It gives the reader information about the author's early life and what he did before he moved to Paris. That in itself was interesting and set the stage for his year in France. The book was entertaining as well. I got a real sense of the author's character and personality. Some of the adventures mentioned, especially the one involving the shady Jean-Paul, were fascinating. I had

the feeling that "Cleef," as his French friends referred to him, never experienced a dull moment in the City of Lights."
San Francisco Book Review – 5 Stars

"Through Simon's crisp, clear prose, the 1980s Parisian nightlife is cast in brilliant relief before the reader's eyes. The costumes, grueling dance routines, casual sex, and dangerous temptations would suit a Hollywood movie, but this is a rare backstage pass to the world-renowned cabaret and a particular era of the city of love. This is a treasure for any Francophile. Simon never dwells long on any particular event, and his memoir moves at the efficient clip of a well-choreographed performance.

While the book includes over 30 pages of photos, these are primarily of Simon rather than of Paris. Simon's Parisian adventures are inlaid within his greater life journey that, while not the emphasis, makes his memoir even more compelling and inspiring. Intentional or not, Simon's memoir *Paris Nights: My Year at the Moulin Rouge* relays a firsthand account of significant historical and social benefit. This memoir should appeal to anyone interested in dance, theater, Paris, the 1980s, the apartheid, or Hollywood actors."
Portland Book Review – 5 Stars

Paris Nights
My Year at the Moulin Rouge

by

Cliff Simon with Loren Stephens

Published by Waldorf Publishing

2140 Hall Johnson Road
Grapevine, Texas 76051
www.WaldorfPublishing.com

Paris Nights-My Year at the Moulin Rouge

ISBN: 978-1-943848-92-8
Library of Congress Control Number: 2015957002
Copyright © 2018

The chapter "White Bubble of South Africa" appeared in a slightly different form in *Crack the Spine*, Issue 159, in September 2015 and was nominated for the 2015 Pushcart prize; and "Diamonds" appeared in the Spring/Summer 2016 edition of *Whistling Shade Magazine*.

This is a work of creative nonfiction. The events are portrayed to the best of Cliff Simon's memory. While all the stories in this book are true, some names and identifying details have been changed to protect the privacy of the people involved.

Front cover design: Darrell Fusaro

To Colette

Thank you for putting up with an actor's life, keeping me humble and giving me more love and support than I could ever have hoped for.

To my sisters Terry and Shelley

And

To the memory of my parents, Mannie and Phyllis, my sister Karen and my beautiful, white British bull terriers, Harley and Montana. You all live forever within me.

In Paris, temptation takes on an entirely different dimension. Those who can resist its sensuality are bound to have died in some sense.

Jacques Riboux, Choreographer

If you are lucky enough to have lived in Paris as a young man, then wherever you go for the rest of your life, it stays with you for Paris is a moveable feast.

Ernest Hemingway, *The Moveable Feast*

Chapters

Chapter 1: The Quest

Certainly a man should travel.
Voltaire, *Candide*

1988

I was feeling restless. My live-in girlfriend Liz and I were fed up with one another. We had been through the break-up and getting back together routine too many times. I loved her passionately, but I was tired of all the fighting.

It was April. I'd wake up in the morning and before I had my first cup of strong coffee, I was bored just thinking about the day ahead. The early signs of autumn (April is autumn in the Southern hemisphere) and the cooler days at the beachside town of Umdloti on the South Africa coast were grating on my nerves; I felt like they reflected my dark mood. When the telephone rang, I barely recognized the voice through the static. It was Gavin Mills calling from Paris where it was already spring. I had met him when he was a dancer at a Las Vegas-type theater in Sun City, South Africa. We never worked in the same dance company, but we hung around together after hours, and became best friends. Both of us were known to be aggressive. Whenever there was a fight in the clubs, the police guessed that Gavin and I were at the center of it. Gavin had served in the South African military three years ahead of me and we both knew how to take care of ourselves with or without a gun.

I had lost touch with him after he'd gone off to Paris, but I heard that he had been dancing at the Moulin Rouge for a year in "Formidable," their latest extravaganza.

"Hey, Cliff, the Moulin Rouge is looking for a replacement dancer in "Formidable." I showed them your picture. They like your looks and you're the right height. What do you think?"

"When do they need me?"

"Now. A dancer broke his leg in the cancan number."

"This isn't another one of your jokes, man?"

"No." He started singing, "April in Paris."

I hung up the telephone, ecstatic that I would be having not one, but two summers this year. Within days I sold my Fiat 850 Spider convertible – full of beach sand – to buy a one-way ticket to Paris. I hadn't saved up any money. At twenty-six, I was still living from day to day with no responsibilities other than to myself, spending whatever I was making on giving Liz a good time and partying as if there was no tomorrow. Our parting was brief. I think she was relieved to see me go. I made no promises to her, but we would eventually see one another again, and each time it would end badly. I needed to sort things out, and Paris was as good a place as any to figure out what I was going to do with my life, and move up in the dance world. I'd had enough of dancing in cabarets in Johannesburg and Durban.

I fell asleep as soon as the plane took off from Jan Smuts airport. At midnight, we landed on the desolate island of Sal, Cape Verde, to refuel. The belly of Africa was declared a "no fly" zone to South African Airways by the black African states. We were prohibited from flying straight north to Europe. Instead, all flights out of South Africa had to fly over the Atlantic circumventing the mainland, which added three hours to the flight time making it necessary to make a fuel stop in Cape Verde, a Portuguese island friendly to South Africa.

Passengers milled about the tarmac, smoking. The moon was high in the nighttime sky, and I could see packs of feral, barking dogs running in the dirt just beyond the runway. Somewhere in the distance, waves were lapping against the island's coast.

Reboarding the plane, I thought of this inhospitable place as a stepping stone out of darkness into the City of Lights. Closing my eyes the words of Karen Blixen in her *Letters from Africa* came to mind: "I felt that Paris was illuminated by a splendor possessed by no other place." I couldn't wait to find out if this Danish baroness was telling the truth.

When the stewardess announced our arrival in Paris, I grabbed my backpack and waited to clear through customs. I was traveling light, and had nothing to declare. The customs officer asked me, "Any diamonds, Monsieur? Any gold?" I thought, *He must be kidding. I don't own a thing in the world.*

It was early morning, but Charles de Gaulle airport was already busy with international travelers. I couldn't understand the announcements, but it was thrilling to hear "Berlin," "Prague," "Barcelona," over the loudspeaker. I felt as if I was at the center of the universe. I looked around for Gavin. He had promised to pick me up. A tall blonde-haired guy approached me. He looked like Dolph Lundgren, the Swedish actor who played the villain in a Rocky Balboa movie. He asked "Monsieur Simon?" I hesitated and then nodded. I was feeling very vulnerable. *How did he know who I was?* He asked me to follow him, took me by the arm, and led me down a dark passageway toward a door, which looked like the entrance to an office building. I thought *what the hell is going on? Where's Gavin?*

I heard footsteps behind me and then Gavin yelled out in his unmistakable South African accent, "Cliff. It's Gavin. Where do you think you're going, man?"

"I don't know."

At the same time, the Swede was pulling my arm. I said, "What the fuck are you doing? Let go of me." I was getting ready to punch him out.

Gavin burst out laughing. He had set me up. The whole thing was a joke. I should have suspected something from the beginning because Gavin was always looking for a way to fool around. "Calm down, man. This is my buddy Joachim Staaf. He is one of the principal performers at the Moulin Rouge."

Joachim gave me a big bear hug. "Welcome to Paris, Cliff. Gavin has told everyone in the company about you."

"Like what?"

"That you're a damn good dancer, that you have a short fuse and a way with the women."

"Guilty, as charged on all counts."

Gavin threw my bag into the backseat of his Mini Cooper and headed for his apartment. Gavin had offered to let me stay with him and his British girlfriend, Sally, who was a dancer at the Moulin. Gavin acted as my tour guide as he maneuvered his car through the busy morning traffic. "This is the La Chapelle area; we're in the eighteenth arrondissement. It's not very chic, but it's cheap and lively, and not far from the Moulin Rouge.

Walking distance in fact. Very atmospheric."

He stopped in front of a gray, Soviet-style building. It didn't look the least bit French to me. He took my bag, and we climbed the stairs to the third floor. He and Sally had a tiny, one-bedroom apartment without much of a view at 10 Rue de La Madone. The next street over was the Rue de la Rose, which had majestic, old-world buildings with arched windows, so there was hope that I would feel like I was living *la vie parisienne*.

I was grateful to have a place to stay since I had no money. Gavin and Sally were living like gypsies, and they were perfectly happy to give me some real estate in their living room. Sally pointed to the sofa, "Hope that's okay with you. That's where you'll be sleeping." I didn't bother unpacking. I just dropped my bag on the floor.

I had arrived.

Gavin and Sally had to leave for work. Gavin showed me the route from Rue de La Madone to the Moulin Rouge on a fold-up map. The first show started at nine p.m. He told me to meet him backstage before the curtain went up, that he'd introduce me around, and then I could catch the show. It was a long walk, but I didn't want to waste my money on a taxicab, and there was no Métro stop near the apartment. I wanted to get the feel of the city, and there is no better way to learn about Paris than to walk its streets.

At dusk, I followed Gavin's directions from his apartment down Rue Marx Dormoy, descending downhill to Boulevard de Rochechouart, named after the abbess of Montmartre, which becomes Boulevard de Clichy in the Red Light District of Pigalle. Looming over the district was the Basilique du Sacré-Coeur keeping a watchful eye over the passing scene, its white cupolas dominating the hillside.

It was a warm April evening, and the streetlights were already turned on. Pedestrians were on their way home from work, and the vegetable markets were still open for last-minute shoppers. I passed sex shops and sex shows. Arab-looking hawkers beckoned me to come inside, and there were girls hanging in the doorway of a club, "Paris by Night." I had seen prostitutes in London when I was a teenager but never dressed so scantily and so obviously working the street traffic.

The street smelled of dog shit. Gavin warned me about this and told me to watch where I stepped. At that time, dogs ruled, and nobody picked up their messes. I could also smell freshly baked crepes stuffed with Nutella. Everywhere there was loud disco music playing. It was the 1980s and "Every Rose Has Its Thorn" by the band Poison and George Michael's "Faith" were thrumming in the air.

I felt totally alive and invigorated by the sights, sounds, and smells of the city. I quickened my step, and when I looked up, there was the red windmill of the Moulin Rouge, turning, turning as darkness descended.

The Place Blanche in front of the Moulin Rouge was clogged with tour buses, trucks, and trailers. Stagehands were carrying heavy crates through a side door; a trainer led a horse past the throngs and into the theater. I stood there watching the choreographed chaos and then wandered over to a hot dog stand to get something to eat. I had already been up for nineteen hours since my plane landed at Charles de Gaulle Airport. I was starving. The woman behind the cart was speaking in a friendly tone to her customers. It was apparent that she knew everyone and was a fixture in the neighborhood. I didn't speak a word of French, but I handed her the correct number of francs because there was a placard on the front of her cart.

Tourists were already lining up outside the entrance to the Moulin Rouge. On either side of the front door were huge posters of the showgirls, acrobats, and a crocodile and snake – two of the specialty acts in "Formidable." I made my way to the stage door, and a security guard let me in. Gavin was waiting for me. He was partially dressed or undressed depending upon your point of view. The first dressing room on the left of a long corridor was for the Italian acrobats, the Nicolodi Brothers. We said our hellos and then Gavin introduced me to Monsieur Thierry, the dance captain.

"So nice to meet you, Cleef."

Gavin explained, "I'm going to take Cliff around."

"Great. We can speak later..." He didn't say 'Glad you're here, just in time.' I thought it was strange, but I just followed Gavin into his dressing room, which he shared with the four other principals of the company. Herbie, one of the American principals, was getting into his opening number costume. He had made the rounds of famous, international stages including Las Vegas. I asked him, "Do you like it here?"

"Man, this is the best place you can work. The Moulin Rouge is where every show dancer wants to end up. It's not that we are the best dancers, but it's the most famous cabaret on the planet. Once you've danced here, you have a golden ticket to anywhere else in the world. Where are you from?"

"Johannesburg." *Joey's if you're a local.*

"Like Gavin here. You two look alike. You're not brothers are you – same color hair, same crazy look in your eyes?" He laughed.

"Thanks." I caught a glimpse of the two of us in the dressing room mirror. We did look alike. That would make us an interesting pair on stage. I turned to Gavin, "Where are the girls?"

"I'll introduce you to Debbie de Coudreaux." We walked across the hall. As the star of the show, she had her own private dressing room and a dresser to help her in and out of her elaborate costumes, which were hanging on a rack – each one marked with a number. A tall mixed-race Californian with almond eyes and chestnut-colored hair, she was a veteran of the previous Moulin shows, "Frénésie" and "Femmes-Femmes-Femmes," and earned the title of "Vedette" in "Formidable," which was supposedly developed just for her to show off her talents. She became the longest-tenured star of the Moulin Rouge, surpassing the exotic black artist Joséphine Baker and the risqué Mistinguett.

Debbie gave me a wintery smile and a perfunctory hello. As we left, Gavin whispered, "Don't mess with her. She can be difficult if you get on her wrong side."

"Good to know. Where's my dressing room?"

"You'll be in with the chorus boys. There are eight guys. They're a good lot. They may try and mess with you, but it's in good fun. You'll do fine."

"So long as they don't touch me." I laughed.

Gavin laughed too, "Well you are a good-looking guy. I

wouldn't blame them for trying."

I could hear the orchestra warming up, and it was almost time for the show to start. Monsieur Thierry approached us. "Cleef, your audition is at ten o'clock tomorrow morning."

I tried to stay calm. "Okay."

"We'll see you then." And he walked off.

I was stunned. "I thought I already had the job, man."

"No, you're going to have to audition."

I started to freak out. "Is this another one of your jokes? If I don't get the job, I don't have any money. I sold my car to buy a one-way ticket to Paris, and I have absolutely no way of getting back to Joburg."

"Don't sweat it. You'll do fine. By the way, Thierry told me you should stay for the show tonight. It'll give you a feel for what we do. He's reserved a table for you. That's a good sign. He doesn't usually do that for a dancer who wants to get into the company unless he's really interested. Now, go out front and I'll meet you at the Café Le Palmier across the street after the show. It's a cool scene."

My heart was pounding. I was pissed off at Gavin for misleading me and scared that I wouldn't make it through the audition. I had traveled over 5000 miles, sold everything, and given up the patchwork of jobs I had cobbled together. I had jumped at the chance to dance at the Moulin Rouge without a net, and now I wasn't sure that one would appear out of thin air to catch me. I wondered if my impetuous decision was going to land me out in the cold.

A tuxedoed waiter escorted me through the darkened theater to a premier table. Red velvet curtains hung across the stage. On every table were tiny lights with red lampshades. The room was packed with tourists. Waiters bustled among the tables clearing the dinner dishes, and opening bottles of Champagne, which they nestled into ice buckets. I saw a Jeroboam of Champagne being delivered to one of the tables. A group of Japanese tourists sat right at the front next to the stage. A waiter came over to my table and told me that everything was on the house. Although I felt like I was being treated like royalty, I still had a knot in my stomach.

When the curtains parted, there were twenty or thirty stunning six-foot-tall showgirls with creamy white skin. Many of the dancers were topless, and they all wore gorgeous sequined costumes and carried large feather fans. I had never seen anything like this before; flying carpets which hovered over the audience, rotating sets, and twinkling chaser lights. I had heard about the special effects of the Moulin Rouge, but they were more spectacular than I imagined. At the center of it all was Debbie de Coudreaux, in her red and white bejeweled costume, looking regal and beguiling. What struck me immediately about "Formidable" was its elegance. The performers were flirtatious without being sexual in their moves and gestures. This was not a glorified "peep show;" it was art and magic.

I wanted to be a part of this world more than anything I had ever wanted in my life. The Moulin Rouge felt like home to me, but that was just an illusion. I would still have to earn my way into the company. I hadn't prepared anything for my audition, and I had no idea what was expected of me.

After the show, I walked across the Place Blanche to the

Café Le Palmier (Now named Rouge Bis), where the dancers hung out between and after the shows. There was a lively crowd having drinks inside; some patrons sat outside under the striped red and cream-colored awning enjoying the balmy April evening. I sat down outside and ordered a glass of whiskey to calm my nerves. Looking through the Place Blanche, I saw the tourist buses pulling away, and crates were being reloaded into trucks. The twinkling lights of the famous Moulin Rouge windmill turned around and around. It was after midnight. I had been up for almost twenty-four hours by then.

I was still pissed off at Gavin for misleading me into thinking that I already had a guaranteed job at the Moulin Rouge, but at least, I'd get a chance to audition, and that in itself was pretty "Formidable."

Gavin had still not turned up. I ordered another whiskey and sipped it slowly letting the alcohol mellow me out. I closed my eyes for a moment, and my mind drifted back to a much younger me. I was just twelve years old, caught in the middle of a rainstorm on the Vaal River, my father waiting for me on the shore. I could have drowned, but I made it back safely.

I felt someone shaking me by the shoulders. It was Gavin. "Hey, man, time to wake up. We need to get going. Tomorrow's going to be the best day of your life or the worst."

"Don't I know it."

Chapter 2: The White Bubble of South Africa

The clocks are ticking my friends. History has got a strict timetable. If we're not careful we might be remembered as a country who arrived too late.

Athol Fugard, *My Children! My Africa!*

1974

I looked back at my mother standing on the lawn of our house, the last rays of burning sun making her hair gleam like gold. She waved and then yelled at my father as he backed his brand-new Jaguar out of the driveway. "Mannie, be careful. It's going to start raining soon. Promise me you'll stay off the water if the storm comes up. I don't want Cliff getting hurt."

My father lit a cigarette and laughed, "Your mother worries too much. You know how to take care of yourself, don't you, Cliff?" I nodded and looked out the car window as we passed other big, four-bedroom houses in Glenhazel, a predominantly Jewish suburb of Johannesburg. One lawn melted into another; there was no need for security gates to separate the residences.

Glenhazel was a whites-only neighborhood in Johannesburg. The only blacks permitted in and out of the area had work permits in their I.D. books like our nanny, Peggy, who lived with us in a small apartment separated from the main house, taking care of my three sisters and me. On holidays, she'd go home to the all-black Soweto Township to see her children and her husband who was a member of the African National Congress. He was a tough guy who resented that she worked for a white, Jewish family, but he gladly took her paycheck. My sisters used to hear her bragging about our family to the other nannies:

"Mrs. Simon, she is so beautiful in her new blue dress. Mr. Simon just gave her a diamond pin for her birthday. And Mr. Simon, I swear he looks like that movie star, Omar Sharif."

"Where'd you see his picture?"

"In Mrs. Simon's movie magazines. She lets me look at them."

"You're lucky to work for such a nice family that boy of theirs – Cliff – his going to be handsome like his father when he gets older."

Peggy answered. *"He's wild sometimes. And spoiled. Too many girls in the house. But he's still my baby."*

"You be careful. He'll be indoda *soon. How old is he?"*

"Twelve. He's strong for his age from all those swimming lessons and gymnastics. He's training for the Olympics. That is what his parents want for him."

"Uyaphupha. You are dreaming."

"No. I mean it. You'll see."

"What are you talking about? You brag too much, Peggy. You think it makes you look more important to us, but it doesn't." And then they all laughed and went back to work.

My dad was anxious to get in a good sail before the rain started, so he drove the twenty miles to the yacht club faster than usual. We sped through Vanderbijlpark running a red light, but no one bothered to stop my father. He was lucky that way.

Recognizing my dad, the guard tipped his hat and opened the "members-only" gate. The parking lot was already emptied out; more cautious sailors had called it quits. The air was redolent with humidity and twittering birds flitted from tree branch to tree branch, nature's harbingers of the building storm.

My dad and I slid our fifteen-foot Tempo racing dinghy off the banks of the Upper Vaal River. Mosquitoes buzzed around our heads, and a swarm landed on my bare arms. I refused to wear insect repellant. That was for sissies. In no time, I was bitten up, but I didn't want to complain to my father.

The river water – normally tawny brown from the silt on the bottom of the river (*Vaal* means dull brown in Afrikaans) – was black reflecting the darkening sky overhead; the waves hit the hull as we maneuvered the boat from the shore. We choreographed our movements so as not to bump into one another in the tight quarters. I adjusted my life jacket, pulling it close into my body.

We reached the middle of the river, about one hundred meters from shore. My dad yelled at me over the wind. "We're turning around." I didn't want to admit that I was scared, but I felt relieved that we were heading back. I bent down as the boom swung around, the ropes strained against the force of the wind.

My dad jumped out of the dinghy. I asked him, "Shall I pack the sails?"

"No, I want you to take the boat out again without me this time."

The rain had started, and I could hear thunder from the west, coming from the mouth of the river.

"Dad, there is a storm coming. I can't handle the dinghy

by myself."

He shouted at me. "I want you to sail to the middle of the river and back. You can do it."

He had a look on his face that left no room for an argument, but I persisted.

"What if I fall in?"

He slapped me on the back. "You're a good swimmer. What have all those lessons been for? If you end up in the water, you can swim back to shore. Don't be a mommy's boy."

That was it. I pushed the dinghy back into the water. Shivering and shaking from the cold, I grabbed the tiller and ropes. In the distance, a bolt of lightning hit the water. Fear gripped my throat, but I had no choice but to keep going. I didn't want to disappoint my dad. I made it to the middle of the river. Struggling to stay in control despite the rocking of the boat, and the ferocious wind, I managed to turn the boat around and get back to shore.

My dad stood at the edge of the water, his white shorts soaking wet, and his thick, black hair plastered to his head from the pelting rain. He leaned over and helped me pull the boat in. We folded the sails, heavy with rain water, and stuffed them in a canvas bag, following our usual post-sailing protocol. He didn't say he was proud of me or hug me. He wasn't a demonstrative man, but he wanted to teach me a lesson, which has counted for more than any words of praise: *"Face your fear, and you can do anything."*

In the shelter of the Jaguar, Dad lit a cigarette and turned on the radio. The announcer reported that "The President of the United Nations General Assembly has ruled that the South

African delegation can no longer participate in the work of the Assembly."

I asked my dad why.

He grunted. "Apartheid. The African countries represented in the UN are all against us, and they're pressuring the other members to join them. The United States has already put sanctions on us, and it's going to get worse. Watch – one of these days, South Africa will be totally isolated, and it will be time for us to get out."

I was too exhausted from my ordeal to carry this discussion further. Silence hung between us. Then my dad looked at me. "Listen, Cliff. Do me a favor. Don't tell your mother what happened today. If she gets wind of it, she'll make a fuss the next time we want to go sailing. It's just between us boys, right?"

"Right, Dad."

"One more thing. Don't say anything to Peggy. She tells your mother everything about what goes on with you. She can't keep a secret."

By the time we got home, my teeth were chattering, and my skin felt like ice. All I could think of was getting into a hot bath. I dropped my wet clothes on the tile floor and sank into the steamy water, reliving the adrenaline rush that came over me as I fought the wind on the river and pulled the dinghy ropes tight between my wet hands. I couldn't believe how strong I felt in the midst of my fear.

I got dressed for dinner. Peggy was in the kitchen making supper. Despite my dad's admonition, I was bursting to tell her about my adventure. I was very proud of myself.

Peggy was wide-eyed and happy for me. "So the lion took you out and taught you how to hunt, my baby."

"I guess so." And then I shared every detail of our adventure with her – maybe even embellishing it to tell her how courageous I had been.

My mother overheard our conversation, and at dinner confronted my father.

"Mannie, how could you have put our only son in danger? He could have been hit by lightning, or fallen out of the boat."

My sisters looked down at their plates and held their breath hoping my father would say the right thing and avoid a fight.

"But he didn't, Phyllis. He is strong enough to take care of himself." That was about as close as he ever got to giving me a compliment. My dad had a nervous laugh when he knew he was in trouble with my mother and was backed into a corner. He smiled sheepishly and winked at me. We were partners in crime.

My mother picked up the dinner bell and rang it to summon Peggy to clear our soup bowls and serve the first course, *boboti*, a typical South African entrée, a spicy version of shepherd's pie. My dad tried to charm my mother. "You have turned Peggy into a gourmet cook, Phyllis."

My mother was on to my dad's game. "Tell Peggy, not me." We finished supper in silence. I went to my room and opened my Hebrew book. On the right page was the Hebrew and the left was the pronunciation written phonetically in English. My job was to memorize the portion of the Torah reading for my bar mitzvah. I soon lost my concentration and put the book away.

I crawled between my freshly-laundered sheets. The storm had finally blown over, but I could hear the raindrops falling off the thick foliage around the house. Down the hallway, my parents were arguing. I suspected that their fight had something to do with what had happened on the river, but I wasn't about to tiptoe in the dark to listen in. Their fights were becoming more frequent. I almost wished they would divorce, but that would mean the end of our family as I knew it. And then I might have had to take sides, which would have been impossible because I loved my mother and father deeply for different reasons. I realized I was crying what my father would have called "crocodile tears." If he had walked in on me, he would have been horrified, and my mother would have been heartbroken. I buried my head in my pillow and finally fell into a deep sleep.

Years later, as my dad lay dying in a hospital in Durban, I reminded him of the day he forced me to sail our racing dinghy into the storm by myself. He smiled weakly and laughed. "That was to have been our little secret."

I told him "It's because of what you taught me that day that I am where I am today. You taught me not how to be fearless, but how to overcome fear. It's a lesson I take with me everywhere. I want to thank you for that, Dad." Then I leaned over and kissed him. Those were the last words I said to him. That night I had to fly to London for work, and he died the same night.

Chapter 3: Leaving Johannesburg
Free Mandela! Hang Vorster!
Student Rioters

Every morning before leaving for school, I would go into the aviary my dad built for me on the back lawn of our house. I bred cockatiels and Indian ring neck parrots and by the time I turned thirteen, I had six pairs of birds. I'd let them stand on my shoulders or my head, and they liked to nibble on my earlobes. I was exclusively in charge of them – my father thought I would learn to be responsible by taking care of them. I'd feed them and clean out the aviary. When the pairs had babies, I used to sell the little chicks to other people in the neighborhood. I'd repeat words to them, and taught them how to speak after a fashion: Hello, Goodbye, Cliff – which they mimicked as "If-If-If". I whistled at them, and they learned little tunes. I loved my birds because they had wings and could fly free, but I had to keep them caged. They were not native to South Africa and would not have been able to defend themselves against local predators.

I used to say goodbye to them before I left for school, assuring them I would be back. I felt part of nature when I spent time with them.

My nanny Peggy used to watch me from the kitchen window, always with a smile on her face. I wondered if she felt like a bird in a cage, wanting to fly free, but afraid to do so. After all, where would she go? I often wondered how she felt about taking care of us while her own children were tended to by relatives in Soweto. I never asked her and I never heard her complain.

In addition to my birds, I also had a pet dog, which was mine alone – a beautiful golden Labrador retriever. My mother picked her out for me and surprised me one day by hiding the puppy in the car under a jacket when she picked me up from swim practice at school. "Look under the jacket, Cliff. There is something for you." I pulled the jacket away, and there was Honey. I loved her to death. From my mother, I learned what it was like to feel unconditional love for another living being.

I attended Sandringham High School in the northeastern suburb of Johannesburg for students from grades eight through twelve who lived nearby. There was no such thing as bussing, so the school was homogeneous racially and economically. It was an all-white, co-educational English-speaking school modeled after the British educational system. (The first black students were not admitted to the school until the 1990s when apartheid ended.) Corporal punishment was tolerated for even minor offenses such as talking in class, wearing your hair too long, fighting or missing sports practice. I got caned more than once, hit with a cricket bat, or whacked with a hockey stick on my behind, which did not upset my parents – if I misbehaved I got what I deserved and I should just "man up." Or at least, that is what my father told me. I am not so sure my mother was in favor of this, but she did not go against my father.

Sandringham had excellent sports facilities including a 25-meter swimming pool, where I competed against one "house" or another. My swim record from primary school through the two years I was at Sandringham was unbroken for ten years. I was seen as a swim phenom and was encouraged by my coaches and my parents to choose swimming over gymnastics, and to prepare myself for international competition.

At thirteen, I had my bar mitzvah at an Orthodox synagogue in Johannesburg after studying for a year with the rabbi in a desultory fashion. I didn't understand a word of Hebrew, but I was enough of an actor that I read my Torah portion for September 7, 1975 (the date of my thirteenth birthday) with some authority, and made my parents proud. Neither my mother nor my father were more than "High Holiday Jews," but as their only son, I was expected to make this passage into manhood. Standing in front of the synagogue congregation, I was very proud of my accomplishment.

My dad's family was originally from Lithuania and had immigrated to South Africa before the Second World War. I know practically nothing about his personal history, except that he was born outside Johannesburg and lived on a farm. The family suffered financially and eventually the family's situation was so dire that his father left him on the doorstep of an orphanage when he was four. My dad's last memory of his father was watching him drive away in a pickup truck. He never spoke of his parents or his lonely childhood. I think it was just too painful for him, but it motivated him to do well in life.

My mother's childhood was somewhat more privileged. Her family were Jews from Poland. She was born in Johannesburg in relatively prosperous circumstances and had the education of the upper class. She had beautiful manners and knew how to set an elegant table. My father was rough around the edges, but this quality made him irresistible to my mother – to all women, in fact. My parents made a handsome couple among the Jewish elite of Johannesburg. My dad was always the life of the party, proud of his glamorous and intelligent wife, but he had the reputation of being a "lovable rogue." My dad made a lot of money in the computer business, but his financial success was undermined by the political and economic turmoil in Johannesburg.

As Jews, my parents always believed in giving back to the community. When I was fourteen, my mother suggested that she and my father become foster parents to a kid from the Jewish orphanage, Arcadia, in Johannesburg. Shani Krebs, who was a few years older than me, used to come and spend weekends with us. He was wild and used to try and beat me up, but it was all in fun. I liked it because I felt like I had a big brother, after all the time at home with three sisters. My family was very fond of him, and I believe that my father was especially sympathetic toward him because he had lived in an orphanage, too. Shani's parents were Jewish Hungarian refugees. When he came over to our house, we shared a room. I'd sleep on the floor, and he'd take my bed.

My parents were afraid that the anti-Apartheid movement would turn the city into a war zone. The Soweto Student Uprisings in 1976 against the Vorster government ended in terrible bloodshed with more than 200 students and adults killed by riot police. The riots were incited by the government edict that all school lessons be taught in Afrikaans, the language of the oppressor, not in English, which meant that the black students had to spend all their time learning a "foreign" language at the expense of their basic studies. Other punitive measures followed as the ANC ratcheted up its militant activities against white power for years to come.

I remember the day that Peggy's husband, who was a member of the ANC, came to our house. He didn't want her working for us any longer and started pushing her around. My father intervened and punched him in the nose and told him to get off our property. Peggy defied her husband and stayed in our employ for a while longer, but when we left South Africa for London, she couldn't go with us. I cried my eyes out. So did she. I had known her from the time I was a baby.

"Cliff, I love you like you are my own son."

I asked her, "What is going to happen to you?"

"Don't worry about me. I'll be fine. I'll find a job with another Jewish family. The Cohens have inquired about me. They got news that your family is leaving."

I felt a pang of jealousy, but I didn't say anything. She continued," I want to hear that you will be swimming in the Olympics someday, don't you know?" She had ambitions for me, just as if she were my own mother.

My dad predicted that things were only going to get worse and that he might not have a "pot to piss in." He felt that the South African economy was collapsing and that everything he had achieved could be taken away in an instant. In his mind, he held the specter of Eastern Europe where so many Jews before 1939 thought things would get better for them, and instead they were tragically annihilated. He didn't want to wait for the same thing to happen to us. He thought that Jews were always the most vulnerable group in society, anywhere in the world. He disagreed with what the government's policies were and didn't want his family to be part of it any longer.

My dad made arrangements for us to immigrate to England, which was a bold move. He would have to close his business and start all over again. We had no family or friends there – just the promise of a safer life. When we left, the South African government allowed my family to take a million rand, the maximum permitted. This was equivalent to $100,000. It's still like that to this day.

And there was another compelling reason for our exodus, which involved my future safety. My parents knew that when I turned seventeen, I would be drafted into the military. It was mandatory for me to register by the time I was sixteen for future enlistment, so if we left when I was fifteen, there would be no record of my existence, and there would be no way that the military could track me down. I'd be thousands of miles away. I was my dad's only son, and he'd be damned if I'd be sacrificed in defense of apartheid. Both he and my mother wanted me out of harm's way.

My two older sisters Karen and Shelley, who were in their twenties, chose to stay in Johannesburg rather than go with us to London because they had serious boyfriends; my youngest sister Terry and I left with our parents in 1977. We wanted Shani Krebs to go, too, but he was already registered to serve in the military since he was about to turn eighteen.

We all worried about what might happen to Shani once we left. He did not have anyone to advise him or show him the love that my mother had showered upon him, other than his sister. He got involved with drugs and the wild life after his military service. In 1994, he flew to Thailand where he was arrested for heroin trafficking and was sentenced to death at the age of thirty-four and sent to Bangkwang Prison, better known as the "Bangkok Hilton." His sentence had been commuted to one hundred years, but he got released after eighteen years, and I'm happy to say that he is back in Johannesburg and is a talented artist and public speaker to teenage groups arguing against the use of drugs. In 2001 while still in prison, after hearing of my mom's death, he painted an amazing portrait in her memory. It still hangs on my wall. Shani chronicled his imprisonment and release in his memoir, *Dragons and Butterflies,* which was published in 2014. We have reconnected, and I call him Brother.

Home was now a two-storey attached Tudor-style townhouse in the Finchley section of north London. The weather was rainy and gray, day after day, and I was totally miserable. I missed the hot, dry heat of Johannesburg, the wide expanse of green lawns, my nanny Peggy, and my classmates, but most of all I missed my golden Labrador Honey. It almost killed me when I had to say goodbye to her. Heartbroken, I gave her in safekeeping to a cousin at my father's insistence. He told me I could not take her with us because there is a six-month quarantine in England for domestic animals. I also found a home for my birds with a breeder, but I had it in my mind to acquire at least a few pets once we were settled in London.

My dad made me apply to Christ College, a secondary, all-boys school in East Finchley. The school was housed in a turreted, red brick building constructed in the late 1800s. It reeked of old English tradition. I saw boys walking around with gray blazers and gray caps. Uniforms and conformity, and worst of all I thought, *How am I going to meet girls at an all-boys school?* The school motto was "Advance All the Way," and the message to parents was that if your boy did well here, he was guaranteed a ticket to Oxford or Cambridge. That was why my dad was willing to pay the hefty tuition. As his only son, he wanted me to succeed in life, and he viewed a fancy education as a ticket to my future success. In his mind, he envisioned that I would be a "professional" man: a lawyer, a doctor, or a financier. He saw these professions as a sure bet. He wanted to give me the privileged education that he did not have growing up, and he was proud that he had the financial wherewithal to give it to me.

My mother and I met with the headmaster of Christ College. He mentioned that the boys at my level were already taking trigonometry. They were way ahead of what I had been studying in Johannesburg. I don't think I did very well on the entrance examination. When I got home, I told my father, "There is no way I am going to that school. And I probably didn't get in anyway."

In less than a year's time, we moved to Edgeware, which was a step up from Finchley.

I ended up at Orange Hill, a comprehensive school in a tough neighborhood, at the opposite end of the social spectrum to Christ College. Most of the students were on welfare and lived in government housing; I sometimes got into street fights, but I felt more alive there and, of course, there were girls to flirt with when I had the time. I made friends easily. My two closest pals were Santosh, an Indian boy, and a black, Nigerian girl named Sami. They must not have known anything about South African whites and apartheid, or they might not have wanted to be my friend.

I always hated school. I resented being cooped up in a classroom; I'd fidget and look at the clock just waiting for the bell to ring. None of the academic subjects really interested me although I was good at math and science. I just didn't have the patience to sit down and read a book, or memorize facts about history – especially English history.

My main focus during high school was on swimming. I planned to train for the 1984 Summer Olympics, which were going to be held in Los Angeles. I joined a private swim team called Barnett Copthall. I'd get into the pool at five in the morning and swim until seven. Then I'd have breakfast and be at school by nine. I had permission to arrive late. I'd go back to the pool during lunch break, and then end my day back at the pool and return home after dark. On average I trained six hours a day, every day.

By 1979, I qualified at the British Olympic trials. I was the seventh-fastest swimmer for all age groups: 1 minute 9 seconds in the breaststroke and 59 seconds in the butterfly at a distance of 100 meters – both categories required explosive speed, rather than long-distance endurance. I was the youngest member on the international British swim team when we competed in Toronto, Canada, against the United States. I did well, but I was not in the top three, which showed me I needed to up my game to medal in the 1984 Olympics.

My mother made it possible for me to follow my rigorous training regime, sometimes driving me to and from school, while my dad supported the family by working for an insurance company, Quid Each Day (QED), which he started from scratch. He used to make me drop QED flyers into peoples' mailboxes to drum up business the old fashioned way – door-to-door. At that time, my mother was also working. She wasn't the kind of woman who wanted just to be a housewife and mother; she valued having her own money, which gave her a sense of independence.

My dad was a serial entrepreneur, but he was not very good at managing the money he made. It slipped through his fingers like water. I heard arguments between my parents about his profligate ways. He was somewhat of a gambler with his investments, and a ladies' man. My mother became disheartened, and I sensed that she missed Johannesburg as much as I did. She was also worried about how my sisters were faring in the midst of the escalating fighting between the ANC and the ruling National Party in Johannesburg. The news from home was bad.

To establish a feeling of normalcy in London, my dad built me another aviary. I got myself a crow I named Bertie. He was extremely smart, but he didn't like me or any other males. I don't think he knew the adage, "Don't bite the hand that feeds you," because he used to act very aggressively toward me. In his mind, there was room for only one male in his aviary, and he was it.

My mother hired a young Swedish girl to help around the house. Bertie loved her. Actually, so did I; she was my first real crush. We would take Bertie out of the aviary into the garden, and he would lie flat on his stomach with his wings spread wide, and she'd stroke his neck. He was in bird heaven.

One day, I put him back in his aviary, and another crow appeared from the park which backed up to our house. The bird flew over our roof and landed on top of the aviary. The two crows screeched and hollered at one another in a noisy mating ritual. This went on for a week. I spoke with Bertie, "You're lonely, right?" He just looked at me and cocked his head. With a tear in my eye, I said, "Go join your friend. I can't keep you caged up just for me. Spread your wings and fly." I walked out of the aviary and left the door ajar. Bertie hopped onto the lawn; his friend landed beside him, and the two birds took off screeching. They hung around the house for two days and then disappeared into the woods. I was happy for them.

My dad sensed my discontent with London and arranged a vacation for the family in Fuengirola, Spain, a small beach town on the Costa del Sol, hoping that a week in the sunshine would lift our spirits out of the fog my mother and I were in. I remember sitting next to him on the hot sand, the waves gently lapping against the shore, and the sound of seagulls calling overhead. As the band played a corny American love song on the patio of the hotel, a beautiful girl walked by us in a revealing white crochet bikini.

I must have been staring at her because my dad said, "Why don't you speak to her the next time she walks by. She is obviously flirting with you, Cliff." I took the bait and spent the entire night on the beach with Andrea. I learned that she was eighteen, a year older than I was, and from Germany. She was lovely and took my virginity with great enthusiasm, passion, and finesse. I will always be grateful to her, and to my dad, as well, for urging me to get on with it. After all, I had been thinking about sex for at least three years, if not longer.

At the beginning of my last year at Orange Hill, one of my swim teammates went to the University of Texas on an athletic scholarship. I thought I should take my training to the next level, and my parents applied for me to go to Southern Methodist University to train with a team called the Mustangs, which at the time was the best team in the United States. I also applied to the University of Texas, at Austin, and both schools offered me full scholarships. I knew that if I took advantage of one of these opportunities, my chances of getting to the Olympics would be greatly enhanced. But something was bothering me.

Early one dreary London morning, I pulled myself out of the pool. I smelled the chlorine and heard the coach's whistle urging my team members on. I had been training in London for three years without a break, and I was sick of it, and I hated the freezing cold weather. I just couldn't get back into the pool. My coach, Rick Bailey, who had led the Women's British Swim team to the 1976 Summer Olympics, sat down next to me. He put his arm around me. "You're going home aren't you?"

I nodded. "I am just burned out. I'm going back to South Africa to enlist in the military. I can't take the life here any longer."

Rick couldn't believe that I would actually walk away from everything that I had accomplished including a scholarship to a United States university. He had high hopes for me, and his reputation was riding on my performance. He had invested a lot in me, foregoing time with other talented swimmers, because he believed I had it in me to stand on the Olympic podium.

I said, "I'm sorry, coach, but I'm done." Just like that, my dreams and years of training came to an abrupt end. I knew I could have medaled, but I didn't care, and I didn't really care that I would disappoint so many people who saw my potential. I just needed to be free.

My parents were shocked. My mother had been my swimming coach when I was a boy, and it was she who encouraged me in swimming and gymnastics. And what was worse, now I was going to do the very thing that my parents had tried to avoid by moving to England – join the military in South Africa. I was stepping right back into harm's way, and there was no guarantee that I'd make it out alive.

But at seventeen, I was not to be dissuaded. I wanted to go back to Johannesburg and test myself against the rigors of military life. I didn't give much thought to the dangers of war or why they were fighting. I was after adventure, and I thought that I was invincible. And there was something else. For better or worse, South Africa was still home to me.

Chapter 4: The Military

"Ad Astra per Aspra." A rough road leads to the stars.
Motto of the South African Air Force

After I graduated from the Orange Hill Comprehensive School in London in 1979, I went back to Johannesburg alone and lived with my cousins until my mother and dad flew back in January 1980. My dad and I drove north to Pretoria, the administrative capital of the country so that I could enlist in the Air Force. Military headquarters were located in the Union Building, atop Meintjieskap, the highest point of the city. In front of the building were terraced gardens with luxurious plantings. The jacaranda trees were in full bloom. Through my eyes, the city was celebrating my enlistment into the military.

I needed my dad's permission to enlist, and he obliged. I think he was secretly proud of me. He didn't want me to be a mollycoddled, spoiled Jewish boy, and he figured that I was physically strong enough from my years of gymnastics and swim training in high school to handle myself. I applied for entry into the Air Force as part of the July 1980 intake. During my two years of service, as an elite athlete, I was selected for the Air Force swim team, competing against army and navy. I received the Victor Ludorum medal two years in a row presented to the sportsmen at the top of their field. For that reason, I often got preferential treatment – which I took full advantage of – but these awards didn't shield me from severe punishment when I openly disobeyed Air Force rules. I could take the punishment, but I couldn't stand it when my squadron mates were taken down with me for a major infraction.

After my dad signed the papers giving me permission to enlist in the military, he went back to London. He was still trying to make a go of things with his startup, Quid Each Day, and he was just two years away from earning his British citizenship, something he had been contemplating.

Times were a lot worse in Johannesburg than when our family moved to London in 1977. Internally Communist sympathizers had organized a powerful movement and had allied themselves with anti-Apartheid factions within the country. There were many white Jewish intellectuals who participated in these alliances.

Countries neighboring South Africa, who had gained independence, were susceptible to Communist propaganda and military influence. The ANC's armed wing, uMkhonto weSizwe (MK), had established a base in Angola invited into the country by Southwest African People's Organization (SWAPO) and the Popular Movement of the Liberation of Angola (MPLA). The Soviets armed all the militant factions, which banned together against South Africa. In addition, there were also 35,000 Communist Cuban troops allied with Angola fighting on the ground. The Cubans left trails of cigar smoke for miles in the bush and were easier to track than an elephant. They were like sitting ducks, and they didn't resist when our troops surrounded them.

This wasn't just a black/white civil war any longer, but an international war fueled by Communist ideology. And into the mix was control over South Africa's diamonds, gold, and cheap labor. The stakes were high.

South African Prime Minister Botha (known as *Die Groot*

Krokodil, which means The Big Crocodile in Afrikaans) was playing a dangerous game: giving some concessions to the blacks while placating the conservative ranks of the dominant National Party. There were strikes in the automobile and mining industries, and more than 100,000 students staged a boycott. In Pretoria itself, the High Court sentenced nine blacks to seven years imprisonment on charges of training as guerrillas in Angola, and the ANC bombed a police station right in the heart of Johannesburg. The U.N. Security Council called for "the release of all political prisoners, including Nelson Mandela and all other black leaders with whom the [South African] regime must deal with in any meaningful discussion of the future of the country."

Despite the political unrest in South Africa, my mother decided not to return to London with my dad. A few months earlier on the flight from London to Johannesburg, she wrote a poem, which she shared with me: *How do I feel? / I am torn and fragmented. / My thoughts jump and fly from one country to another. / Where do I belong? Must I belong to someone?* She wanted to be close to my two older sisters, who had stayed in Johannesburg. Her poem foreshadowed my parents' eventual divorce, which was all for the best. She did not say so at the time, but she might also have thought that by staying in Johannesburg while I served in the military, she could guarantee my safety – magical thinking on her part, but understandable. She loved me deeply and could not fathom losing me to distance or a terrorist's bullet.

Most of the new recruits met in Johannesburg at the railroad station and boarded a troop train to Pretoria where they were then trucked to the Air Force camp in Valhalla for basic training. (I always thought it was a perverse name for a camp – in Norse mythology those soldiers chosen by the Valkyries who die in battle are sent to the Great Hall of Valhalla).

My mother insisted on driving me to the camp. At the time, I thought it was ridiculous but looking back on it, I realize that she just wanted to delay having to say goodbye to me, and face the reality of being alone. (My dad was back in London, and my sisters were getting on with their lives.) We drove the forty-minute trip in silence; my mother was trying to prepare herself for our separation, and I was "chomping at the bit" to test myself against the other recruits and prove that I had what it took to excel in a brutal environment. We both got out of her car at the security gates. I grabbed my gear, and said, "I love you Mom." She held me tight. I turned away quickly and walked through the gates not wanting her to see that I had tears in my eyes. I could feel her standing there until I disappeared into the intake office to report for duty.

I was expected to serve in the military for two years, but after just three weeks in basic training, I thought, *what the hell have I done? I've had enough*. I had made an impetuous decision and had not given much thought to the realities of military life with its strict rules and regulations, the grinding routine and daily threats of punishment. It was a lot worse than the rigors of swim training, which I was trying to escape, and the bleakness of London.

I got a weekend pass and told my mates that I was heading for Germany to see a girlfriend I had met in Spain. I was expected back within two days, but I didn't show up until Tuesday midnight. I was AWOL. When I knocked on my instructor's door to report back for duty, Corporal Maclean just stared at me. Then he took me down to my squadron and made everyone do punishment PT. He physically beat me in front of the entire group calling me *fokken Jood* (fuckin' Jew), which I had heard aimed at me and other Jewish recruits in the camp since my arrival. He went at me the entire night. I just kept smiling, trying to taunt him. Actually, in a perverse way, I enjoyed the punishment – it was exhilarating. I felt the same adrenaline rush I experienced when my father challenged me to sail solo into the storm on the Vaal River when I was twelve years old. I was trying to prove to myself that I could take it and that I was not a weakling.

I was covered in my own blood, but I wouldn't let Corporal Maclean get the better of me. After that incident, I think I earned his respect, and he earned mine, but he gave me fair warning. "If you do this again that's it. You're going to detention barracks, and you'll spend the next two years in a jail cell." This was the first time I fully realized that there were serious consequences for my actions. Not only was I getting beaten up for breaking the rules, but on other occasions that I rebelled I took my buddies down with me, and that bothered me more than anything else.

Over the next few weeks of basic training, things were going well between us. Then one morning Corporal Maclean came into my tent with something on his mind. There was a little patch of grass peeking out of the sandy floor underneath my cot. He kicked my cot over, and tipped my cupboard over, too, which held all my beautifully folded and ironed shirts. All my possessions were in disarray. Now I would have to wash and iron everything over again. I followed him out of the tent. I was furious, but I spoke with him in a very polite tone and called him sir, as I was expected to do. I said, "Sir, I want to be here. I volunteered to be here, but that patch of grass under my bed is staying. It's not going to be gone, and you can come back tomorrow and do the same thing, and it will still be there. I am not pulling it up." He never did it again.

Our instructors came up with all manner of torture and surprise to harden us for the realities of the battlefield. To get us in shape, they'd tie a wooden box filled with ammo packs of R1 rounds weighing about sixty pounds around our necks and make us run up and down hills on the firing range for an hour in the 100-degree heat. The box dug into my neck, and I could feel the blood running down my back. A lot of the recruits – myself included – ended up puking their guts out or fainting.

As a special surprise, our instructors told us, "We're going to throw smoke grenades onto the field, and all you have to do is get through the smoke." When the grenades exploded, they left behind a huge white cloud. The instructors yelled, "Run." I took off, but within seconds of hitting the cloud my skin started to burn, and I couldn't breathe. I realized that I was running through tear gas. I closed my eyes and just kept running. The gas stuck to my skin, which was covered in perspiration, and my lungs felt like they were on fire. A lot of the soldiers became totally disoriented. We used to have to do this over and over again. I eventually became desensitized to the tear gas – which was the point of the exercise.

Conditions in the Pretoria tent camp were deplorable. We

had no hot water for showers; toilets were drop holes in the ground. Meals were served on *vark panne*, a pig plate, which had three sections for the food. The plates were always greasy because we had no hot water to wash them in. We used to get up at four in the morning and train for sixteen hours. Lights out at eight p.m., and then up again at four am into the below zero freezing cold morning air.

Shortly after I completed three months of basic training, I had the evening off. I went to a bar in Johannesburg with some buddies, and we all got very drunk. A fight broke out on the street. I got jumped from behind, and I back fisted one of the guys, sending him flying right over a car parked at the curb. I was amazed at my own strength and couldn't believe how tough the military had made me in just a few months. I had never hit anyone before. I was impressed with my newfound strength.

The military was a great leveler – it didn't matter if you were a rich kid from Johannesburg or a farm boy from the Free State. All recruits were white, and we were all treated the same. At that time, blacks were not allowed to serve in the military; they could hold down civilian jobs such as cooks or janitors on the posts, but were not trusted to carry a gun.

The way to get through basic training was to keep your head about you – it was really a mental game, and some of the recruits couldn't stand the pressure. The military philosophy is to break you down, and then build you up. Sometimes, things go wrong when you are at the lowest point and most vulnerable. About six months into training, one of the new recruits, who was still in basic training, committed suicide.

Like all new recruits, he was given an R1 rifle, but he was not allowed access to bullets. Somehow, he stole ammunition from the stores and then blew his brains out. I was told to go into the tent where he had shot himself. Another recruit and I were supposed to clean up the mess. There were fresh bloodstains and brain fragments everywhere. The top half of his head was gone. We rolled up his body in a blanket, carried him out and swabbed everything down. The whole episode was totally shocking to me, and I threw up for the rest of the day. We found a letter he had written to his girlfriend's mother telling her that her daughter had broken up with him, and he hoped she was happy now. He was just a kid, seventeen or eighteen, and emotionally unstable – like a lot of us.

At the end of basic training, parents were allowed to visit their sons at the Valhalla Base before they got their assignments. The soldiers started lining up inside the gate at dawn's first light. Dressed in their military uniforms with their hair cut short, a lot of the parents couldn't even spot their own son. More than one soldier would chase after a car, and just like a little kids, yell out, "Mommy, mommy." Quite funny, in a sad way. My mother and I spent a few hours together. I tried to make light of the grueling routine. I didn't want her to feel sorry for me. That would have just made everything worse.

After basic training, we were required to pull guard duty once a week. I was assigned to guard the stores where the ammunition and weapons are kept. I was on the midnight to six a.m. shift, a time when marauding bandits from the city often tried to break in and steal what they could. I heard a noise. I walked around the corner. It was pitch black. I switched on my flashlight and held my rifle at the ready. I spotted a black man hiding in a gully. The beam of my flashlight caught his face. His eyes were like two saucers. I don't know who was more terrified, him or me. I was shaking. That was the first time I had drawn my weapon on someone. I tried to stay calm and managed to handcuff him. He was armed, so I was lucky he didn't draw his weapon and take a shot at me. I took him back to the guardroom at gunpoint where he was locked up. I don't know what happened to him. He probably was thrown in jail for a few months. For me, this incident made me realize that we had an enemy – the threat to our lives was real, and not just something our instructors kept drilling into our heads.

When I enlisted in the Air Force, my dream was to become a jet fighter pilot. I can still remember as a boy flying radio-controlled model airplanes with my dad. We used to take our planes and fly them above the lawn behind our house in Johannesburg. My dad had a friend who built some of the planes for us, and the two of us started to build them ourselves. Of course, I used to crash them a lot, which made my father very angry, and we ended up spending more time repairing them than flying them, but it was fun for me and gave me a chance to have my dad all to myself without my mother and sisters vying for his attention.

All I could think about when I enlisted was getting into the cockpit of a French Mirage F1CZ. With its speed and firepower, the Mirage had overtaken the Soviet MIG-21s in combat. The idea of being in command of the Mirage was intoxicating, and it was all I could think about. The Afrikaners called the Mirage the *Vlamgat* or Flaming Hole, and their pilots were *Vlammies*. They were at the top of the Air Force hierarchy; with my competitive spirit, that was where I wanted to be.

I went through the pilot selection process with high hopes. There were 800 applicants a year; 20 per intake are selected for training and out of the entire group two, or at most three, qualified. Not very good odds. The commander told me, "If you want to be a jet pilot you're going to have to learn to speak Afrikaans. All communication is in Afrikaans. It's a security thing." I only had three months of language training, which was hardly enough to put me in charge of a fighter jet.

He indicated that I had a good chance of making it if I went to language school. I told him, "No way. I've had enough of school." I couldn't see myself sitting in a classroom. I was too restless, and frankly, by the time I was in the group of twenty candidates – I wanted to see some action in the field.

I got assigned to the munition stores at Valhalla Air Force Base – maintaining the R1 and R2 rifles, which are similar to American M-16s. I had a Star 9mm sidearm on me at all times; I liked the feel of a gun in my hand, and I was a good shot. I was working in the stores at the tent camp stocking the shelves and checking equipment. One of the lieutenants came up behind me, yelling *"Fokken Jood, Fokken Jood."* He grabbed me by the throat. He thought he was being funny. What an idiot. I smacked him hard, and heard his head hit the ground. His head was bleeding. He looked up at me completely shocked that I would haul off and hit him. I screamed at him, "What are you doing? Don't you ever touch me and don't ever call me that again." Anti-Semitism and bigotry were rife in the military. In

South Africa there was no such thing as "political correctness" – every insult was tolerated, and that was particularly true in the military.

The commanding officer gave me two choices for my actions: go to detention barracks for three months, which is the standard sentence for assaulting an officer, or take PT punishment right then and there. I said, "No way am I going to jail." I was marched out to the parade grounds, and the flight sergeant who ran the detention barracks was waiting for me. He had a bad reputation; it was rumored that when he was enforcing PT on a recruit in detention barracks six months earlier, the boy had a heart attack and died. The flight sergeant was never disciplined.

Flight Sergeant Dick Head kicked me hard in my ribs, which dropped me to the ground, and then proceeded to press his boot on my head; he made me crawl around on the gravel. And all the time he was yelling at me, "You're worthless. You're no better than a dog." He stayed on me for three hours pushing, kicking and slapping me. I was covered in blood and crying with anger. Afterward, I took a cold shower and put on a clean uniform. Later in the day, the bigoted lieutenant who I had clocked came up to me. He wanted to shake my hand. "Friends?"

I told him to get away from me, but a few months later, we were back on good terms. It was all part of the military's philosophy that soldiers had to respect authority, endure insult and injury and follow orders at any and all costs because in the heat of battle there is no tolerance for insubordination. This was a turning point for me. I proved to myself that I could withstand the abuse and not crack under pressure. They could beat me, but they couldn't own me or break my spirit. It actually made me stronger, so thank you to Flight Sergeant Dick Head for changing my life for the better. I grew up three years in three hours. If I was being honest with myself, I was a bit of a spoiled Jewish brat, and I didn't really respect authority. I needed a wake-up call, and I got one from Flight Sergeant Dick Head.

I'm glad that the lieutenant I hit and I had a rapprochement because he was killed on a reconnaissance mission across the border into Angola. I would have felt terrible if I never got around to making peace with him before he died. He was just doing his job – trying to make a better soldier out of me.

Occasionally, I got assigned to a four-man helicopter crew. Our job was to bring weapons up to the front lines at the border. We'd gas up at Swartkops Air Force Base across from the Valhalla training base, fly as far as Ondangwa, which is in Southwest Africa [renamed Namibia after the fall of apartheid], and fifty miles south of the Angolan border. Oshakati and Ondangwa – which had been around since World War I – were our two forward bases on the border where soldiers would congregate. There were also smaller, secret camps for the Special Forces deployed on the ground across the border.

We were very vulnerable riding in open helicopters flying at low altitude, about 500 feet above the ground. The guerrillas on the ground – who were being trained and equipped by the Soviets – shot at us; we couldn't see them, but we took aim at whatever moved. This was bush warfare. Because we were in the Air Force and not on the ground, like the army infantry grunts, some of the other recruits used to call us pussies, but it was usually said in jest, because they relied on us to ferry supplies back and forth. Fortunately, I didn't have to remove any of the wounded or dead soldiers. That was left up to the MEDEVAC teams.

Occasionally I'd be sent up to the border in a Nord C-160, a huge troop carrier. This was the ultimate rough ride. In order to avoid being shot at by the insurgents on the ground, the plane would fly high and then take a nosedive straight down for the airfield instead of gradually losing altitude, the idea being to get down as quickly as possible. When I was a new recruit, the officers used to shove us in the back of an open truck and ride roughshod over the bumpiest terrain, to prepare us for a flight in a Nord C-160, which they fondly referred to as a Flossie. If you weren't careful, you'd bite your tongue off or crack your head against the side of the truck.

The South African military brainwashed the troops into believing that we were fighting a just war against terrorists. To this day, I feel like a fool for having believed this. I didn't give much thought to the fact that there were five million whites and thirty million blacks in the country. I blindly accepted that "white is right." The country's economy was built on the backs of blacks – all the diamond and gold mines were manned by black workers who were paid next to nothing while the whites got rich. The British colonials had been there first and now the Afrikaners, who pushed the British out during the Boer War – were in charge of the body politic. One white master was simply traded in for another, all in the service of controlling the country's abundant natural resources and keeping a boot on the heads of the black majority. But times were changing, and the younger generation of whites was starting to question the status quo. It would all play itself out in the years to come. Eventually, the power would shift from the white minority to the black majority, but in the process, there would be bloodshed and mayhem in the streets and in the bush.

Chapter 5: Cabaret

Conformity is the jailer of freedom and the enemy of growth.
U.S. President John F. Kennedy

I thought about staying in the military as Permanent Force, but after two years and achieving the rank of lance corporal I had had enough of the white supremacist attitudes and being called a *Fokken Jood* at least once a day. I didn't want to press my luck. I signed my discharge papers on July 31, 1982, and said hello to freedom and liberty.

I was twenty years old, and I felt like my life was just getting started, but I had no idea what I was going to do. With 800 rand in my pocket (the equivalent of $80), I said goodbye to my parents, put on a backpack, and traveled around Europe stopping in Munich to see my fantasy girlfriend, Andrea, who by this time had taken up with someone else. He was jealous and didn't want me hanging around with her, knowing that we had had a seaside fling in Spain.

In my travels, I saw men and women – black, brown and white – mixing freely with one another, making love to one another, and even getting married, which would never have been tolerated in South Africa. In fact, it was against the law. Interracial couples had to meet under the cover of darkness, and if they were caught, they were often tried and thrown in jail. I knew that there were interracial salons in Johannesburg and elsewhere among artists, musicians, journalists, and philosophers, but I was never exposed to this because my parents were rather parochial and isolated themselves within their white segregated Jewish milieu.

From Europe, I took a plane to Tel Aviv, where my sister Terry was living with her husband, an Israeli, who was involved with the country's security services against its Arab neighbors. The wish to fly jets was still in me, so I spoke with my brother-in-law Eli about joining the Israeli Air Force. I thought I could just step into pilot training, but he informed me that I'd have to repeat six months of basic training in the Sinai Desert in order to qualify. His exact words to me were, "Do you want to run up and down sand dunes in blistering heat?"

"Definitely not." That was all I needed to hear to squelch that dream and move on with my life.

I came back to Johannesburg from Israel and picked up random jobs. I really had no direction. Coming out of the military, I was happy to just live without anyone telling me what to do. On a lark, I headed for Durban to a resort on the Indian Ocean where I got a job teaching windsurfing and water skiing at the Umhlanga Sands Hotel. The ocean was generally off-limits to the guests except at lifeguard spots. The waves were enormous, sometimes reaching thirty feet and sharks trolled the water. I'd go down there by myself on my days off and body surf and swim where I wanted to. I didn't give much thought to the sharks, and they didn't show any interest in me.

I lived in a little apartment on the water in Umhlanga, a short walk from the hotel. On clear mornings, I could see dolphins jumping in and out of the waves, and in June and September, whales migrated off shore.

The atmosphere at the resort was like a Club Med, and as an employee of the hotel, I was expected to mingle and socialize with the guests and teach water sports. One of the guests asked me to service his wife. She was gorgeous, so I didn't mind too much. He walked to the beach with his children, carrying sand buckets and toys, and signaled to me that the coast was clear, and I could go up to their room. One of my buddies was not so lucky. He had taken an interest in the wife of another guest. While the two of them were rolling around in bed together, her husband started banging on the door. He leapt from the balcony with nothing on and landed right in the swimming pool. Being in my early twenties, single and carefree, this was all just great fun.

The Beverly Hills Hotel, which was down the beach from us, had a nightclub with a cabaret act. One of the dancers convinced me to try out for a part – they needed a male acrobat. I had never been on stage before, but she convinced me to audition. I showed up in board shorts and a tank top. I was sun-tanned from all the time working outdoors, and I was in tip top shape from windsurfing. I did a few continuous *flic flacs* in perfect form, handstands and tight spins, which I learned in gymnastics. The choreographer Neil McKay stopped me. "Great. We want you in the show." And that was it. When I went on stage in front of a live audience, I thought, *This is what I want to do*. I loved the applause, and when I smiled at the audience, they always smiled back. It felt like the most natural thing in the world, and although I had not yet developed a stage presence, I could see that I was making a positive impression on the customers.

Eight months later, I went to work at the Millionaire's Club in Durban and moved to another beach town, Umdloti.

I was the only male dancer and shared the stage with three beautiful girls, which I didn't mind at all.

There were more than a few nights that I got into trouble. Sometimes guys in the audience, thinking I was gay, got clever with me. Whenever that happened, a crunching roundhouse kick to their heads stopped them in their tracks. The police knew that if there was trouble at the club, I was usually at the center of it. One night, guys who were on the police rugby team, came into the club. My parents were there with my live-in girlfriend, Liz. As we were all leaving the club, one of the cops grabbed Liz's backside. I laid into him, hearing his rib crack as I shot my fist into his chest. No one moved, and then the police were called. I was put in the back of a police van and they threw tear gas at me. I didn't care. I was trained to deal with tear gas in the military, so that it wasn't a big shock to my system, although it feels like your skin is peeling off your face. I said, "Are you finished?" And that was that. The Rebel in me grew.

I had another run-in with the police. After my dad's hernia operation, I took him for a doctor's appointment in Johannesburg. Liz was in the car with me. I dropped him off in a "No Parking" zone in front of the doctor's office. As I pulled out into the road, the driver behind me started honking his horn to let me know that I had been parked illegally and was blocking traffic. My dad started yelling at him from the curb, and the driver gave my father the finger. I threw my car in reverse, stepped on the gas, and blocked him from moving. I jumped out of the car and smashed the driver's window with my hand. By this time, I was out of control. I pulled the guy out of the car, head butted him, and felt his nose break, all the while screaming, "Fuck you, you bastard. Get out of here." His faced was covered in blood. I shoved him back in his car, and he drove away, but not before his girlfriend took down the number of my license plate. I saw my father walking slowly into the medical building, the stitches across his stomach biting into him with each step he took.

I drove off. All of a sudden, I was overcome with guilt for having hit the guy. I started to shake and tremble. I pulled into a car park, and broke down sobbing, regretting what I had just done. Liz said, "Cliff, you aren't in the military anymore. You can't act like that." "I know. I couldn't help myself. He was being rude to my dad, and I couldn't let him get away with it. But you're right. I overreacted." I didn't know it then but I'm sure I had PTSD.

I received a call from the police. "Mr. Simon, you need to come into the station. You've been charged with assault and battery."

I was not surprised, but what happened next was totally unexpected. I walked into the police station. The detective recognized me. He said, "We need to discuss what went on. The guy you smashed in the face got your license plate number. He wants to press charges, and if he does, he'll probably win, and you could go to jail for a very long time."

"Listen, I was just trying to protect my dad. The guy was shouting obscenities at him and it looked like he was going to attack him. He just got out of the hospital. That's no way to treat an old man." Those words caught in my throat, but the truth was my dad was getting older, and I saw the early signs of the frailty that would ultimately take him down.

The detective looked at me. "Man, I would have done the same thing. I'm going to tell the guy to drop the charges." Only in South Africa.

I thought of the police in Durban as trigger-happy cowards. A lot of the guys who completed basic training with me were allowed to opt out and go into the police force rather than stay in the military.

It wasn't unusual for the police to harass women just for the sport of it. One night, while I was performing in Durban, I got a telephone call from my father. He was at the la Lucia police station with my girlfriend, Liz. I could hear her sobbing hysterically in the background. I told my father to put her on the phone. "Liz, what's going on?"

"I couldn't get ahold of you, so I called your father to help me. I was driving back to our apartment. A cop on an unmarked motorcycle was following me. He pulled me over and asked me to hand over my car keys for no reason. When I said no and wanted to see his police ID he got very aggressive. He dived into the car and tried to grab my keys. I fought him off, but he scratched me up. I don't know what to do."

"I'm coming over there right now."

My dad had warned the captain that I had a temper and knew how to use a gun. The captain took him at his word, and when I got there, the cop responsible was nowhere to be found. I was in a rage, but none of the police came near me to try and calm me down. Liz agreed to drop the charges, but I was prepared to go to jail over what had happened to her.

A few months later, Liz's close friend, Steve Lawrence,

who was a police officer in Durban, ended up killing his girlfriend. Michele Thomas was a celebrity in the dance world and had won the 1981 World Championship in freestyle disco. She was the sweetest person and everyone who knew her loved her – myself included. Steve was jealous of her and monitored her every move. In the middle of a rehearsal at the Wildcoast Sun Hotel where Michele was performing, Steve broke into the theater and started yelling at her. He told Michele that if she didn't come outside with him, he was going to shoot all the dancers in the company. (She had forewarned the hotel security that there might be trouble, but they did absolutely nothing to protect her.) He dragged her into his car, pulled out a gun, killed her, and then shot himself – not once – but twice in the head. The murder-suicide made the front page of the *Sunday Times* and completely shocked not only the dance world but the entire country. I couldn't believe that someone so unstable had earned himself a place in the police force. After that incident, I lost what little respect I had for the police and didn't trust them "as far as I could throw them."

I moved back to Johannesburg where I got myself an agent and started modeling and appearing in music videos. I was working constantly and making very good money, but I knew that you can only go so far in Joburg. I wanted to play a bigger game. I dreamed about going to Hollywood someday, and appearing on television and in feature films, but I knew that walking down the catwalk in an Armani suit, and appearing on the cover of local magazines, was not going to get me there. I was still working in clubs, but I had graduated from doing acrobatics to dancing. I worked at a classy dinner theater called La Parisienne (shades of things to come) in Braamfontein, a central suburb of Johannesburg in the thick of established, old theaters and nightclubs between Jan Smuts Boulevard and Empire Road.

Driving home at night, I used to keep a loaded shotgun on my lap, the barrel pointed toward the door in case there was trouble. I also wore a snub-nose 38 special strapped to my ankle. I knew I couldn't rely on the police for protection against thieves and gangs. I was a product of the gun culture, and I was not afraid to take the law into my own hands if I had to, although I had no burning desire to kill anyone. I had seen enough dead bodies in the military to last me a lifetime. There was always a chance that you could get caught in a terrorist explosion. No place was off limits – buses, the City Hall, army transport were all targets of the ANC and other splinter groups. The streets were no longer safe, and car bombings were a daily occurrence. The anti-apartheid movement was gaining strength, and the Afrikaner government was losing control. It was only a matter of time before the National government would have to cede power to the black majority in order to try and stop the violence.

One night, after finishing a show, a limpet bomb exploded in a trash can just down the street from the club where I was working. I saw the flare go up, the air shock waved around me; I was close enough that I could have been killed. Before the police could barricade the area, I jumped into my car, and gunned the engine, getting through just before the barricades went up.

* * * *

I had not seen Peggy, my former nanny, in four years, and I missed her terribly, but my work schedule had made it nearly impossible to visit her. We finally reconnected. She was working for a white family in my mother's neighborhood of Hyde Park taking care of three children and running the household, as she had done for us. Peggy showed me her room; on the walls were pages torn out of magazines with me in advertisements and on stage at the Millionaire's Club and La Parisienne. I realized that she had been following my career, and was obviously proud of my accomplishments, even if I wasn't standing on a podium receiving a gold medal in swim competition at the Olympics. In her eyes, I was already a celebrity.

Peggy put her hands on my shoulders. "Cliff, I was so worried about you in the military. Your mother was too, but I am sure she didn't say, did she?"

"She always worries about me, no matter what I am doing or where I am. It gets to me sometimes. Why is she like that?"

"Every mother worries about their children, if they truly love them. I worry about my children all the time. My oldest boy is fighting in Angola for the MK right now. His father made sure of that."

I thought, *How ironic*. A few years earlier I had been fighting against the MK. But for a quirk of timing, I could have been aiming a gun at him. Peggy had named her son Cliff, after me, and her two daughters after my older sisters, Karen, and Shelley. That is how much she loved us. I wondered how she had managed to convince her husband to allow her to do that, since he hated us, as he hated all white people.

She sighed. "I pray every night that my son will be safe, just like your mother did when you were gone."

She took a handkerchief out of her pocket – as I had seen her do so many times – and wiped her eyes. She hesitated for a moment and then continued. "There is something you should know about your mother, which will help you understand why she worries about you."

"What's that?"

"She lost two babies before you were born. So when you came along, she was so happy. And then, there was the accident."

"What are you talking about, Peggy?"

"When you were just two or three, your mom told your sister Terry to watch you. She went into the house. You and your sister were playing on the lawn. You ran away from her and fell into the swimming pool. I was standing at the window like I used to do. I yelled for your mother, 'Help, Mrs. Simon. Help.' You almost drowned. Your mother jumped straight into the pool with all her clothes on and saved you. I don't think she ever forgave herself for leaving you alone with your sister."

"Did she tell my father?"

"Oh, he was angry like a rhinoceros. You know how he can be sometimes."

"This is the first I've heard of this."

"*Ni ukerli*. It is truth. A big house has its secrets."

I needed a minute to absorb what Peggy told me. The story put my mother's exaggerated concerns about me in a different light.

We joined the lady of the house in her spacious living

room. The furniture was covered in chintz, and there were heavy taffeta draperies on the windows to ensure privacy and insulate the room from the heat and cold. Mrs. Cohen said, "Please sit down, Cliff. I'll make some tea." I could tell that Peggy was uncomfortable sitting there dressed in her maid's uniform. She was not used to receiving company in someone else's house. I asked her, "Are you still married, Peggy?"

"No. My children are old enough now, so I divorced him. He doesn't own me anymore."

"I'm glad to hear that."

"And what about you, Cliff? Do you have a sweetheart?"

"No. I don't want to be tied down to anyone."

"Well, you have time. Twenty-four is young for a man. Not for a woman. It is a good thing that your three sisters are married. Your mother loves being a grandmother."

"Marriage is not for me, and having children is out of the question. At least for now."

As if on cue, one of the other maids brought an infant into the living room. Peggy held her in her arms and rocked her gently. The baby smiled and cooed.

Mrs. Cohen said, "Peggy has the magic touch. Whenever the baby gets fussy, I just give her to Peggy. We are very lucky to have her working for us."

I wanted to tell Peggy that she could do better, that she should explore the world, and not just trade one cage for another. Instead, I said, "You know I was in Europe for a while after I got out of the military."

Both women nodded.

"It was amazing to see blacks and whites mingling freely.

Even going out with one another."

Peggy raised her eyebrows.

Mrs. Cohen touched the back of her neck and tucked a few stray blond hairs into her chignon. "We are not ready for this in Johannesburg. We probably never will be."

At the risk of irritating her, I said, "That's not true. Someday, when Mandela is released from prison, and the ANC gains a seat at the table, things will be different. Until then, South Africa will be a country in turmoil, and the international community will continue to ostracize it."

Mrs. Cohen cleared her throat. "More tea, Mr. Simon?"

"No, I better be going. Thank you for your hospitality, Mrs. Cohen. You have a lovely home."

Peggy walked me to the door. I held her tightly. She whispered in my ear, "You will always be my favorite, my baby. Don't be a stranger."

I saw Peggy again when I returned from the Moulin Rouge, and then at my mother's funeral in 2001. After that, I lost touch with her. Eleven years later, I was at a party in Los Angeles. One of the guests was a young South African girl from Johannesburg. She came up to me and said, "Hey you're Cliff Simon. I recognize you. You starred in that television series, *Egoli*.

"Yes."

"Peggy was my nanny. She used to tell me all about you and your sisters."

I couldn't believe my ears. This was the Cohen baby Peggy had taken care of when I visited her in 1986. "Do you know how she is? I always wanted to get her out of South

Africa and bring her to the United States, but we lost touch with her after my mother died."

"I don't think she would have wanted that. South Africa was always her home, for better or worse." She hesitated and then continued, "I'm sorry to tell you that Peggy died last year. She had cancer. Her life was a hard one, no matter how well we whites treated her. " Both of us started crying. Hearing about Peggy's death was just as painful as when I sat with my mother holding her hand as she took her last breath. My only regret is that I never showed Peggy how life should be. I still think of her every day as I do about my parents, and my eldest sister, Karen. They are all my angels, and I know they are watching over me.

Chapter 6: Audition

Don't forget. A great impression of simplicity can only be achieved by great agony of body and spirit.
Boris Lermontov, *The Red Shoes* (1948)

1988

Gavin Mills drove me to my audition at the Moulin Rouge the morning after I arrived in Paris. He parked Oliver, his Mini Cooper on the sidewalk just past a cabaret theater I had walked by the night before when I arrived from a long flight out of Johannesburg. The club was called, "Paris by Night" where you could hire a prostitute for the price of a cup of coffee. I got out of the car and looked up. The white travertine of the Basilique du Sacré-Coeur glistened in the morning light.

A dark-skinned girl – probably in her late twenties or early thirties – wearing a pink mini-skirt, tight black sweater, and net stockings approached us on the street. "Bonjour, Gavin. You're up early."

"I might say the same to you, Chantal."

"Slow night."

"*Tant pis.* Maybe you'll make it up tonight."

"Let's hope so. Who's your friend?"

"Cliff. He's visiting me from my hometown for a few days. I'm showing him the sights."

She put her hands on her hips. "Does he like what he sees?"

She laughed. I could smell tobacco on her breath, and a whiff of cheap perfume.

I wanted to be on time for my audition at the Moulin Rouge, so I tried to cut the conversation short, "Nice meeting you."

She stood her ground. "My name is Chantal Ortolan. I'll be around this evening if you come back to Pigalle. Look me up. I can show you a better time than this guy."

Gavin interrupted, "Listen, Chantal. Cliff's probably going to be joining the Moulin Rouge Company, so he's off limits."

"*D'accord,* but if you don't get in, just remember – Chantal Ortolan."

I followed Gavin down the alleyway behind the Moulin Rouge at 82 Boulevard de Clichy. He pushed the stage door open, and we were encased in darkness. Gavin said, "Chantal's harmless enough, but the guys around her aren't. You played it just right." He put his hand on my shoulder to guide me through the warren of corridors and storage rooms. Ropes and pulleys hung everywhere; mustiness seeped into the air from the walls original to the building, which dated back to the late 1800s, when the Moulin Rouge was part of Paris's demi-monde of wealthy businessmen who rubbed shoulders with laundresses, dancing the cancan to show off their blanched petticoats. (Some of the girls didn't bother to wear pantaloons.) Fresh hay mixed with the odor of horse droppings filled the corridor backstage as we walked into the theater.

I could feel the adrenaline pumping through my body, and the muscles in my legs were twitching. I kept trying to calm myself down by taking deep breaths, and telling myself: *Performance anxiety is just the flip side of performance energy. Use it.*

I had on a pair of leather jazz shoes, pants, and a tank top to show my body. Monsieur Ruggero Angeletti, who trained the male cancan dancers, and Doris Haug, the artistic director who was in charge of the famous Les Doriss Girls and supervised the choreography for the show, sat mid-theater waiting for me. I did a few back flips, splits and squats in the wings to warm up.

Gavin stood on the side of the stage as I took my place. Doris tapped her clipboard with a pencil. "Okay, Cleef, show us what you've got. Do *un chassé, un pas de bourée,* and then *une double pirouette.*" I had taken some ballet classes in Johannesburg, but I was by no means a ballet dancer. I looked at Gavin, terrified, but he was not about to rescue me.

I asked Doris to show me what she wanted. I was a bit thrown off my game because an artistic director or choreographer usually shows you the steps and expects a dancer to copy them. At least, that was what I was used to. But then again, this was Paris – the big time.

Doris got up from her seat and climbed onto the raked stage, demonstrating the steps. I copied her; as I turned, the boards creaked under my weight, and had less spring than I was used to, but I managed to execute the moves without embarrassing myself. Then Monsieur Ruggero joined us. He wanted to see how high I could kick. He said, "That's good enough. You'll learn how to do better in my class." I was feeling encouraged. Then I did some *flic flacs,* somersaults, splits and handstands to show them what might set me apart from the other boys and earn me a place in the chorus.

While Monsieur Ruggero and Doris conferred with one another, I held my breath. My fate was in their hands. After what seemed like an eternity, Monsieur Ruggero told me to be at the Moulin Rouge at nine the next morning for my first cancan class. He didn't directly say, "You're in," but I was.

I woke up at first light and dressed quickly and quietly so as not to waken Gavin and Sally, who had worked late the night before. I ran down the stairs and grabbed a croissant and a cup of coffee at the boulangerie on the corner of Rue de La Madone. The display case was practically empty by 8:30 a.m. Most locals were already at work. It was turning into a cloudy day; the sky promised rain, but I felt excited and elated.

Every new recruit into the Moulin Rouge is expected to take Monsieur Ruggero's cancan class regardless of their experience – even the best dancers, and I was by no means one of the best. I had gotten by in South African cabaret on my looks, stamina, and agility. Now I was in a different league and had to prove that I was a real dancer and top notch performer.

"Are you ready, Cleef?" Monsieur Ruggero clapped his hands.

"Yes."

"This will be two weeks of hell, but you will thank me at the end of it. I will get you ready to go onstage."

I thought, *What could be worse than basic training in the South African military?*

He had a wooden chair in front of him. "Now, you will do roundhouse kicks over the top of the chair." As I stretched to clear the top of the chair, he dragged it, and I continued. I must have repeated this move, at least, thirty times. He signaled me to go higher, and by the end of the class, I was kicking over his head. The goal was to kick with your leg right next to your ear and over your head in the air; alternating left and right.

After my first class, I had to climb a flight of stairs back to the dressing room. I could barely make it. My legs were burning, aching and numb all at the same time. I had been dancing for six years straight in South Africa, and kept up my gymnastics training, but nothing had fully prepared me for Monsieur Ruggero's cancan class. In between the kicks, we'd do stretches, front splits, and side splits. If you didn't keep this up every day, your flexibility goes, and your body will fail you right in the middle of a performance. And that can't happen if you want to avoid injury and keep your place in the show.

After two hours of torture, Doris told me to get dressed. She was handing me off to Madame Jacqueline, a spirited, petite blonde woman fondly referred to as the "Documents Lady." We were going by Métro to the police Préfecture at the Ile de la Cité for my work permit. The train swayed back and forth. I had to hold on to a strap to keep from falling over. The noise of the wheels grinding along the track underneath was deafening. We changed trains and exited at Cité in the fourth arrondissement, just as the bells of Notre Dame rang in the noon hour.

The Préfecture was just to the west of the Cathedral. We walked past the throngs of tourists taking photographs of the stone portals, statues of the kings and apostles, and the enormous rose window. A *bateau mouche* floated past the

Cathedral on its journey up the Seine River.

There was a long line of applicants waiting outside the Préfecture. Jacqueline said, "Come with me. We don't need to stand in line."

"Why?"

"The Moulin Rouge gets priority treatment from the Préfecture because we are a major employer in the city, and so they help us as much as they can to expedite work permits. On that note, try and stay out of trouble. You have the Moulin's reputation to uphold. *Compris?"*

"I get it, but don't believe everything Gavin told you about me. He likes to exaggerate."

I followed Jacqueline to the counter. The police officer checked my passport and then handed me a duplicate form to fill out. He glanced at my answers and then stamped my application. My *Carte de séjour* was issued for one year only, from April 1988 to April 1989. When the year was up, I would have to choose whether to stay with the Moulin Rouge, go somewhere else, or return to South Africa. I had no idea what I would do, and I didn't really care. I was just ready for whatever Paris wanted to show me of life. A year seemed like a long time.

* * * *

I made it through the two weeks of Monsieur Ruggero's punishing training and started in "Formidable" as a swing dancer. The choreography was basically the same for the eight male performers I filled in for, but each one was in a different position, so I had to make the adjustment. Sometimes, the routines were slightly different from one part to another. I also had to learn to lip sync the singing parts.

The dance numbers in "Formidable" were choreographed by Billy Goodson, an American originally from California, who worked with the Moulin Rouge for more than twenty-two years. During his illustrious career, he is also credited for creating numbers for Michael Jackson, Paula Abdul and Gloria Estefan, and has taught dance around the world. While I was working in Paris, I never met Billy, but his intricate routines brought me to my knees on more than one occasion.

Each performance of "Formidable" ran one hour and forty minutes, nonstop, with twenty numbers. We had a live orchestra, which was enhanced with recorded music, and recorded singing. Everything was moving so fast that the audience didn't have a clue that some of the singing or music was not live. Whenever I had a break, during the solo and specialty acts, I changed costumes. I wore seven different costumes and with each a different pair of boots or dance shoes. The heels were individually sized for each dancer so that all the men looked to be the same height. (The height minimum for the male dancers was six feet, and for the girls, five feet, eleven inches.) When I ran off stage, I'd just strip out of one costume, and with the help of a dresser, get into the next one. Fortunately, everything was laundered and repaired daily, because my outfits were soaking wet by the time I got off stage.

After the show, everyone in the cast stood on stage while Doris and Monsieur Ruggero read their performance notes. They demanded perfection, and it was up to all eighty dancers to uphold this standard: "Joachim, you were too far stage left in the '*Les Garçons du désert*' number. Sally, watch your right arm. You almost hit Veronique in the eye when you were both under the blue light. Gino, you were two beats behind the music. Just because you've been here for five years, doesn't mean you can get away with being sloppy. And don't forget to smile, smile, smile. You are supposed to look like you are having a good time, and everything you are doing is e-fort-less."

I held my breath, hoping that I wouldn't be criticized. When Doris called out my name, my legs started shaking. "*Pas mal*, Cleef. Not bad." I breathed a sigh of relief, but she wasn't finished with me.

"Have you been practicing your lyrics?"

"Yes, Madame."

"That's a surprise to me. You missed some of the words in '*Allons à L'Opéra*.' "

"What should I say?"

"Say, *Pardonnez-moi*. I apologize."

I was pissed off, but I was smart enough not to mouth off at Doris. "Sorry. It won't happen again." And it didn't.

Chapter 7: Rue Lepic

When a finger is pointing up to the sky, only a fool looks at the finger.

Confucius and used in *Amélie* (2001)

By the end of my first week on stage at the Moulin Rouge, I established myself as a guy you couldn't mess around with. I minded my own business, but if you crossed me, there would be a price to pay, and it wasn't pretty. I still had a hair-trigger temper, which I kept under wraps, but when provoked or pushed around physically or mentally, I reacted.

I was waiting in the wings between numbers with my back to the stage, which wasn't very smart because you have to be aware of what is going on around you at every minute. Dancers are running on and off; heavy scenery is being rolled out or lifted and changed with ropes and pulleys. The stage is small relative to the number of dancers who are literally shoe-horned inside its three walls. There have been no changes to the stage dimensions since the Moulin Rouge was built, which makes it authentic and charming, but difficult for choreographers and performers.

You can easily get killed by a swinging piece of stage business if you don't watch out or knocked off your feet by another dancer. During a performance, Debbie de Coudreaux ran off the stage and bumped right into me. She hit me in the back with her hand and yelled, "Get out of the way." She thought she could do whatever she wanted because she was the star and I was nothing more than a swing performer. I went out on stage, did my number, and then ran straight to her dressing room. I was furious. I banged on the door and didn't even wait for her to answer. I just walked right in as she was changing her costume and said, "Don't you ever fucking touch me again."

"You were in my way."

"I understand but don't you ever touch me again."

She said, "Well, we'll just take this to the boss."

I answered, "Okay take it to Monsieur Clerico. See if I care."

I was prepared to defend myself against her accusations, but nothing happened. I never heard a word about our *contretemps*. It was Monsieur Clerico's philosophy that the cast should work out their problems among themselves. He had bigger fish to fry, as I was soon to learn. This was petty stuff to him. He was in the business of making money in all ways, and couldn't be bothered with arguments among the cast members. He left that up to the dance captains to sort out, and I guess this incident did not warrant their attention.

Word got out about what had happened between Debbie de Coudreaux and me. Everyone in the cast was shocked, but they understood and respected me for standing my ground. Debbie eventually apologized to me, and I apologized to her, and it was over.

Gavin was not the least bit surprised. He told Monsieur Thierry, the dance captain for the boys, "See I told you. Cliff is crazy." But he said it in a way that showed he was proud of me.

In late April the performance schedule changed and instead of one show at nine p.m. with dinner served, there were two shows a night: one at nine p.m. and a late show at eleven-thirty. I was performing six nights a week, with one day off, and making about 15,000 francs a month, which was the most money I had earned in my career as a performer. I could afford to move out of Gavin's apartment, which was a relief to all of us. I am sure that Gavin and Sally wanted their privacy, and so did I.

I found a studio apartment on Rue Lepic, a narrow winding street which climbs up to Montmartre from the Boulevard de Clichy to Place Jean-Baptiste Clément. The street is named after Count Louis Lepic, who fought in the French Revolution and in the Napoleonic Wars. As I became familiar with Paris, I would learn that many of its famous streets are given the names of generals and battles. Paris is very proud of the country's military history. The great French singer, Yves Montand, who appeared at the Moulin Rouge, wrote a song in tribute to Rue Lepic and to its vegetable vendors, comparing their cries to ocean waves.

One day a week, Parisians are permitted to put out furniture onto the street that they want to get rid of. It is a form of recycling, because whatever is left on the sidewalk is picked up by someone else. I furnished my apartment from the curb of Rue Lepic and the furniture district below Sacré-Coeur, collecting a mattress, table, and chair, which I carried up two flights of stairs to my apartment. That was all I really needed to make a home. My studio had a small window opening onto an interior courtyard. I could see my neighbors from the window, and they could probably see me – which made for interesting viewing from time to time. I had a private bathroom with a handheld shower and a bathtub that was so small that I could only sit in it, Marquis-de-Sade style. It would have been a luxury if I could have stretched out my aching legs, but at least I had hot water.

I used to walk downhill to the Moulin Rouge. It would be a few months before I had enough money to buy my Fiat Ritmo, although it was always a problem finding a parking place around Place Blanche, so it was often easier just to walk than drive to work. As I approached the Moulin, I would usually be accosted by one of the pimps on the street enticing customers who had made their way into the Red Light District. I'd always smile, and then say, "Moulin Rouge dancer," and they'd leave me alone. It was an unwritten law of the street that the Moulin performers were never prospective customers for the prostitutes.

After working long hours at the Moulin, and ending the evening with drinks at Le Palmier, I liked returning to the solitude of my studio apartment. Sometimes I'd wander up the cobblestone streets of Montmartre at dawn, buy a coffee and a hot chocolate croissant at one of the cafés that had just opened, and climb the hill past the carousel and the funicular to the terrace just below Sacré-Coeur. The grass was usually still wet with dew. As the sun rose over the gray mansard roofs, the sky turned a soft pink. I could see all the way to the Eiffel Tower. I felt as if Paris was at my feet. All that was needed to complete the scene was a flutist from the Conservatoire playing Jacques Dutronc's "Il est Cinq Heures, Paris S'éveille." Paris is waking up, and I am about to go to sleep.

Chapter 8: A Note

And the whole world madly turning, turning turning 'til you can't see.

Eric Blau, *Jacques Brel Is Alive and Well and Living in Paris*

I earned a permanent place in the boys' chorus after six weeks. Monsieur Ruggero told me, "You're not the best dancer, but you are like Gavin and Joachim. You've got what they have. You dance like a man, and you know how to make eye contact with the audience. You have that *je ne sais quoi*, Cleef." I also was a perfectionist. I made sure that my kicks were straight up over my head, and that my arms were always in the correct position.

Gavin, Joachim and I gave off a bad boy aura on stage, which attracted attention, especially from the women, and we constantly smiled at the audience unlike many of the boys who didn't look like they were having much fun. They were just going through their paces. We used to fool around on stage. One night, during the Viennese waltz number, Gavin was coming off stage as I was going on, and he stuck a note on the back of my white tuxedo jacket, which said "Kick me," in big letters. The patrons closest to the stage could see it, and they started laughing. Thierry danced by me, and pulled it off. After the show, Doris Haug – who watched every show and gave comments to the dancers if they were out of step or didn't hit their marks – wrote Gavin and me up. She warned us, "The next time something like that happens, we're going to dock your pay and the time after that, you'll be out on your asses." But that never happened because Gavin, Joachim and

I were somewhat "untouchable." Occasionally we'd push one another on stage before our cues, or try and trip one another during a dance sequence, but we were good at covering things up. When you are doing the same show twice a night, day after day, you need to do something to amuse yourself, or you get stale, and your performance suffers. The audience is there to be entertained and titillated, and if you become blasé, the audience won't have a good time. I knew this instinctively.

I also knew the importance of making eye contact with the audience. I'd pick someone in the middle of the theater and play directly to them, because a theater director once told me, "If you play to one person, you bring in the whole audience." The first few tables right up against the stage were usually reserved for Japanese tourists. The Moulin Rouge was the last stop on a twelve-hour city tour, and they were usually exhausted by the time the show started. It wasn't unusual to see a whole group – wearing surgical masks to ward off germs – with their heads on the tables or resting right on the edge of the stage. Gavin and I sometimes gently kicked them awake. It was very disconcerting to see them nodding off. It would sap our energy. They also were in the habit of rushing out single-file before the finale to avoid the crowds. As a performer, you always need to work off the energy of the audience. If they are engaged and excited, it makes the evening come to life. Although the theater was dark during a performance, the stage lights spilled out into the audience, and I could usually see what was going on several rows back.

For example, during the can-can number – which lasted a grueling twelve minutes in "Formidable" – I would see the audience's smiling faces immediately light up (even the tourist who had been napping); they'd start clapping in time to the music, and the clapping didn't stop. This was the highlight of the show then, and it still is today. Most of the other dancers on stage never saw the audience's reaction because they were focused only on the back of the theater, rather than taking in the first few rows. They missed a lot, and there was a lot to miss at the Moulin Rouge, on stage or in the theater.

If I spotted a beautiful woman in the audience, I would flick her a note from the stage with an invitation to meet me afterward. It usually worked like a charm, because what woman does not want to meet a straight Moulin Rouge dancer? I tried this with a stunning older woman, who was sitting at a table in the front row next to a gentleman, presumably her husband. As the husband turned away from her, I aimed a note at her, and it landed right on the table. She grabbed it before her husband noticed. After the show, I waited for her at the stage door, confident that she would be there. I was really very arrogant. The applause and the admiration had really gone to my head. I thought, *I'm going to make her day.*

I greeted her with a rehearsed invitation. "Hi, I'm Cliff. How about a cup of coffee tomorrow? I'm free in the afternoon."

She said, "My husband and I will be on a plane back to Chicago by then."

I took a chance. "Well, why don't you meet me at my apartment later? I have to do another show, but I'll be home by two a.m." I wrote down my address and read it to her. "Six Rue Lepic. *Premier Étage*, apartment one at the end of the hall. It's just a few blocks from the Moulin. I'd love to see you."

She took my address, snapped her handbag shut, and walked quickly to catch up with her husband who was looking for her at the entrance to the Moulin. She had an air of mystery about her, and up close she was even more stunning than I anticipated. She was wearing a red silk dress and a diamond necklace; her black hair was in a chignon, and her body exuded a musky, Oriental perfume, which I didn't recognize. And lucky for me, she spoke English, although the language we were about to engage in had nothing to do with words.

When I went backstage, I overheard the dance captain for the girls telling Doris Haug that there was a problem with the plumbing in the girls' shower room. She asked Thierry if the girls could use the men's shower. Gavin and I decided to take advantage of this emergency. After the late show, we stood at the bathroom door and told the boys they couldn't come in. They didn't want to force their way past us, so they waited in their dressing rooms. Four or five of the showgirls marched into the men's communal shower. You could probably fit ten people in there quite comfortably. Gavin and I walked in with them and took our towels off. I said, "I hope you don't mind, but we're showering with you."

Since Gavin and I were straight, the girls were thrilled. The prettiest among them said, "Come right in." We were laughing and grabbing one another and joking around, but there was no sex. In fact, sex between dancers could be a dangerous game. What happened backstage was your business. Management didn't care, but if it affected your performance on stage in any way, you risked losing your job. And a romance gone bad spells trouble.

I was still laughing to myself about this impromptu "shower scene" as I walked home past the sex shops and all-night cabarets of Pigalle. Clothes were strewn around the floor of my apartment, and there were no personal touches except a photograph of my mother and father on a vegetable crate, which doubled as a nightstand. It was one of my favorite pictures of them. They were at the Parthenon in Athens: my father looking relaxed and happy in a white sports shirt, jacket, and sunglasses and my mother wearing a Gucci silk scarf tied around her head à la Jackie Kennedy. Their holiday smiles belied the fragility of their marriage.

I opened the window into the courtyard to let in the soft night air and got undressed. My mattress looked very inviting after four hours on stage. I closed my eyes and began to drift off. I heard a knock on my door. It was the mysterious Madame X. She kicked off her high heels and deftly unzipped her red dress, which pooled at her feet. We made love for several hours. Before she left, she said, "I can't believe I was just with one of the Moulin Rouge dancers." I had no qualms about sleeping with her. Whatever happened between us was her business. I didn't bother to ask her anything about herself. I didn't even know her name. I fell back to sleep after she left. At around nine or ten o'clock in the morning – well before I usually got up – there was a knock on my door again. She asked, "Can I come in?"

"Sure." I was surprised, and I didn't want to risk tackling a jealous husband, although he wouldn't have much of a chance against me. I asked her "Where's your husband? I hope he didn't follow you."

She laughed. "I told him I wanted to take one last walk around Paris before we leave. He's back at the Ritz reading the morning newspaper." We had sex, and then I kissed her goodbye. I never saw her again. All I could think about was, *She'll remember this day for the rest of her life.* I certainly have. Had Madame X come back to the Moulin Rouge that September, she would have been able to say that she had made love with a *principal* performer of the Moulin Rouge, not just a member of the boys' chorus because that was where I was headed.

Chapter 9: Opportunity Knocks

Opportunity may knock only once, but temptation leans on the doorbell.

Unknown

Monsieur Thierry and Doris pulled me out of the boys' chorus and asked me to understudy for one of the principals for two weeks while he was on summer vacation. I could hardly believe my good luck. I suspected that some of the other boys who had been in the company a lot longer than I were jealous of me, but I didn't really care. I wasn't at the Moulin Rouge to win a popularity contest. I was there to make a name for myself. Now I could put on my résumé, "Understudy to a Principal Performer, Moulin Rouge, 1988." I wrote a letter to my father telling him my good news, but I didn't hear back from him. Since my parents' divorce, he had been moving around quite a bit with his live-in girlfriend. I thought perhaps my letters had not reached him. At least, that is what I told myself so that I wouldn't feel angry or disappointed. I just tried to put it out of my mind.

I filled in as the Arabian prince in "The Floating Carpet" scene during my turn as an understudy. I was dressed in a sequined vest, silk pantaloons, and a large feathered turban. I had taken advantage of the backstage tanning bed, so my skin was dark, and I learned to apply my own makeup in such a way that it did not look artificial or garish, but still made my face stand out under the bright, colored lights. Putting on stage makeup is an art – you have to strike just the right balance between nature and art.

As the orchestra and recorded music queued up, I took my position, stage right, on a "magic" floating carpet, which had ropes attached to each corner. The stagehands pulled hard on the ropes, and I floated above the stage and out over the audience. Debbie de Coudreaux was positioned at the opposite side of the stage, and the two of us met in the middle above the audience, suspended in the air. The audience oohed and ahhed. It was a good thing that Debbie and I had made peace with one another, or I would have had a hard time looking lovingly into her dark brown eyes. Suspending performers over the audience was just one of the many innovations of the Moulin Rouge in the 1980s, and it was later copied by musical directors all over the world.

Every song in "Formidable" was in French. I wrote my songs – six in all – phonetically since I still did not speak any French beyond *merci, au revoir* and *comment vous appelez-vous* when I wanted to flirt with a pretty girl. I put all the songs in a notebook, and tape recorded each one. Then I'd ask Gavin, who spoke passable French, "What does this mean?"

"This is an emotional moment. He's singing about his wife or his girlfriend." I made notes next to the lyrics so that I looked like I understood what I was singing about, and I had the appropriate expression on my face. I would have looked ridiculous if I was singing about losing a lover with a smile on my face unless she was a pain in the *derrière.*

Every song was pre-recorded for the show, but you still had to know the lyrics so that you looked like you were singing live. I had the microphone in front of my mouth as I danced, flirted, and moved quickly across the stage through the chorus.

Everything was an illusion meant to fool the audience and create magic.

The principal's voice had been recorded for my solo numbers. The tone and timbre of his voice suited me perfectly, so my two weeks as his understudy were seamless. Monsieur Ruggero and Doris were very pleased with my performance.

When the principal came back from vacation, he had a disagreement with management and wanted to leave the show. He told Monsieur Clerico. "I won't let you use my voice anymore. You're going to have to re-record all the songs, which are mine." He was in for a big surprise. He didn't realize that when he signed his employment contract, he agreed to allow the Moulin Rouge to use his recorded voice in perpetuity whether he worked there or not. So he lost his voice, so to speak, and I inherited it along with a promotion to principal in less than six months. And I did it all without being able to sing a single note or speak more than a few words of French.

At that point, my salary doubled to 30,000 francs a month. I could afford to move out of my little studio on Rue Lepic into a much more luxurious apartment at 82 Rue de la Victoire, which I rented from a dancer who worked at the Lido de Paris, a cabaret on the Champs-Élysées. Her parents owned the building, and she lived across the hall from me. My rent was less than half the going rate because I was part of Parisian cabaret, which was a tight-knit community of locals and expats, and the owners were more than happy to make special accommodations for all of us.

The apartment, although just one room, was so large that I could have fit my Lepic studio in the bathroom, and the tub was big enough to accommodate my six-foot frame comfortably. Oddly enough the shower was located in the kitchen. I could be cooking up some bacon while a gorgeous, naked girl soaped up and rinsed herself off beside me. Needless to say, it could get very hot next to the stove.

In the nineteenth century, the building was a *hôtel particulier* intended for a wealthy Parisian family and its staff of maids and valets. It had double-height arched windows fronting the street and an elegant winding stairway up to the second floor. The driveway was made of cobblestone, and there were heavy wooden doors that swung open wide enough to allow a car through into the courtyard for private parking. On the street level next door was an expensive women's lingerie shop, and a few blocks away near the Place de l'Opéra, was the famous Galeries Lafayette, one of Paris's oldest and most fashionable department stores. Beyond that, the elegant Grande Synagogue de la Victoire.

My new neighborhood reflected my elevated status at the Moulin Rouge. I had stepped out of the low-rent eighteenth arrondissement into the elegance of Baron Haussmann's ninth arrondissement. My street was named in honor of Napoleon's victory in Italy; in earlier times, the area was a swamp and full of frogs, and was called Rue Chantereine, the singing frogs, which amused me, and was quite à propos of my talents in that department. My voice was so bad that I wouldn't even sing to myself.

My name was added to the "Formidable" posters in small type right alongside Gavin Mills and Joachim Staaf, and the other principals, next to the dazzling photographs of Debbie de

Coudreaux, Doris Haug's cancan girls, the Nicolodi Brothers, the comics, and a menagerie of exotic animals whose acts were meant to shock and amaze the crowd and serve as interludes between our song-and-dance numbers.

* * * *

The Moulin Rouge stage was equipped with a large aquarium which was raised and lowered by a hydraulic lift from the basement level. The aquarium accommodated two, eight-foot crocodiles trained by a burly Yugoslav, Karah Khavak. He used to walk out onto the stage and dive into the tank. He'd swim alongside them, and then put his head right into their jaws. I knew something about crocodiles. They have very little muscle strength to open their jaws; ninety percent of their muscles are for clamping down on their prey like a steel trap. Once they have something between their teeth, they won't let go. It was a mystery how they were trained – they must have been very well fed. No matter how many times I watched the crocodile act, I felt a *frisson* of terror and my adrenaline would start to pump. I used to think, *If something goes wrong here, this guy's done for. He'll get eaten right in front of a thousand people.* But it never happened.

Karah and his wife, Marianne, also handled a huge python. She would come out on stage dressed in feathers and dance with the snake to canned music. Then she'd lay the snake down on the stage near the lip so the audience could appreciate its size – it was fifteen feet long, and its skin was black, yellow and brown. The people in the front row automatically recoiled, wondering what would happen if the snake decided to take a little slither. Despite the illusion of danger, Marianne had the snake under her control.

I love wild animals. Growing up in South Africa, I used to take trips into the game parks with my family; from a safe distance, we used to watch the animals grazing in the bush or wading into watering holes. I asked Karah, "Can I go downstairs and see you with the crocodiles and snake?" There were two large pine boxes next to one another, which were used to transport the crocodiles. He opened the lid and very carefully lifted one of the crocodiles out of its box. A dim light emanated from a single bare bulb in the ceiling, creating eerie shadows on the basement wall, illuminating the scratches on Karah's face. The air smelled musty and damp, and the boards of the stage creaked over our heads.

The crocodile's eyes focused on me. Huge sharp teeth hung down from his upper jaw. I was staring into the snout of a primordial killing machine, unchanged from what his ancestors must have looked like thousands of years ago. Crocodiles can go for two years without eating, storing fat in their tails, and when a tasty morsel like me crosses their path, they lurk in the brush and then strike.

As if to test my own bravery or show my stupidity I asked Karah "Can I hold him?"

"Yeah, but be careful, Cleef. Put your arms out and just watch for his tail. If he swings that thing at you, you could lose a leg."

The crocodile easily weighed 180 pounds. He flicked his tail back and forth, but not in an aggressive way. He was just using it to keep his balance.

I asked Karah to take a photograph of me with the crocodile, who was unfazed by the flash bulb. After our photo op, I asked Karah if I could swim with the crocodile. The water tank was right next to us. He turned white and said, "That's not a good idea. You'd just be a little dog treat for him. And I can tell from the look in his eyes, he's getting hungry." He put the crocodile back into his box and took the python out. Draping him around my neck, I could feel his body throbbing, and the weight of him pushing down on my shoulders. A python kills its prey by squeezing it to death. He'll bite you to anchor himself, and then coils himself around you. When you breathe out, your chest contracts. At that point, the snake will tighten his grip, so that you cannot take another deep breath. Every time you exhale, it squeezes tighter until you can't draw another breath and you suffocate. It is a slow and nasty death. It's really an amazing animal. He seemed quite happy with me. On the other hand, I was happy to have him off me. He actually made me more nervous than the crocodile.

At one time, the Moulin Rouge had an act with two dolphins. One of the dolphins was trained to leap out of the water and pull the brassiere off a showgirl, who then jumped into the water and swam topless with them. When the dolphins weren't performing, they were sent on vacation to Antibes on the Riviera. Eventually, Monsieur Clerico cancelled the dolphin act and replaced it with other spectacular numbers. All the animals at the Moulin Rouge are treated very well and are considered part of the family. The animals are used on a rotational basis, so no one animal has to perform two nights in a row – reducing the stress on them. On their off nights, they are at leisure in very comfortable quarters outside the city.

I've heard that Marianne and Karah are working now with the grandchildren and great grandchildren of the pythons who had performed in "Formidable" so many years ago.

The mascot of "Formidable" was Macbeth, a magnificent white Arabian stallion weighing over 1,000 pounds who was trained and ridden by an ex-circus acrobat. Every night, Macbeth would be led through the Place Blanche – to the amazement of the waiting crowds – and into the theater through a narrow stage door. He was kept downstairs next to the boiler room in a cordoned-off area where he waited for his cue. When it was his turn to come on stage for the Arabian number, you could hear the sound of his hoofs clomping on the stairs. Sometimes he'd take them two at a time – he was quite the show horse. His rider would yell out to everyone backstage, "Clear aside. Macbeth is making his entrance." You didn't want him to run into you. He was a horse on a mission.

I played the Arabian prince in the number, and his rider was a stuntman, Pascal, who was the villain of the piece. I'd be standing in a spotlight singing at the far end of the stage in the corner with showgirls behind me. Macbeth would gallop flat out from the opposite side of the stage. Cracking my huge whip, he was trained to stop right in front of me and rear up on his hind legs. Usually, this trick went without a hitch because Macbeth wore rubber booties to keep from slipping on the raked floor. One evening, his front legs slipped; he couldn't rear up, and instead he hit me hard with his front legs. I went flying off the stage and landed on one of the tables smashing all the glasses, feeling my head bounce off the table, waking the Japanese tourists up out of a sound sleep. They couldn't figure out if this was just part of the show. Champagne bottles crashed to the floor. It was a huge mess. I rolled off the table, stood up, apologized, and climbed right back on stage, and finished the number.

My legs were sore for several days. It felt as if a car had hit me. Macbeth was okay, although it must have been a shock for him, as well. But like me, he was a trooper, and we carried on as if nothing unusual had happened. I ran backstage and changed into my silk pantaloons and vest. One of the dressers secured my white sequined turban on top of my head in just a few seconds, and I climbed onto the magic carpet, as Debbie de Coudreaux floated toward me over the audience. As they say, "The show must go on."

I wasn't about to let an understudy steal my thunder. I earned my place as a soloist, but I was always trying to prove that I deserved to be where I was and that I was tough enough to withstand any mishap – even being kicked off stage by a thundering Arabian stallion. Besides, I wanted the attention. It is what kept me going.

In another number, I impersonated the historical figure Aristide Bruant, who opened Le Mirliton in 1885, a famous club in Montmartre. He was known for poking fun at the upper crust guests of his club and used to make jokes while singing. I stood onstage at the top of a stairway dressed in a black poncho, leather boots, bolero hat, and Bruant's signature, red scarf wrapped around my neck. (Toulouse Lautrec made a poster with his image, and the costume department copied his attire down to the last button.) Pointing to the audience with my walking stick, I'd sing *"Voir Paris,"* "Look at all of

Paris, my friends." Of course, I was lip syncing. Waiting at the bottom of the stairs, were forty beautiful showgirls, decked out in their feathers, some in full costume, others topless.

A spotlight followed me down the stairs, and all eyes were on me. I loved the attention. It's what kept me going, but in the back of my mind, I wondered how long I could continue to perform in such an arduous show, night after night, with all the hidden risks that only a performer is aware of. To the audience, it all looks effortless, but it isn't.

Abraham Simon,
my paternal grandfather.

Bem and granny
Mae Silberman, my
maternal
grandparents at the
Langham Hotel,
Johannesburg, 1937.

1951

My glamorous parents, Phyllis Silberman and Emanuel Simon, before their marriage, 1951.

(L-R) Dad, Mom, Pearl and Puxie on vacation, South Coast, Natal.

My proud father with his new Packard car.

Dad on the beach during his honeymoon, beaming.

Mom and Dad at a business excellence award ceremony in which my dad won an award.

Holiday away from the kids, at the Acropolis, in Athens, Greece, 1970.

At 10 years old, with balsam remote control airplane my dad and I made.

The Bar mitzvah boy with Mom and Dad, 1975.

Bar mitzvah day, Front; My sister Terry and me. Back (L-R) My sister Shelley, Mom, my sister Karen and Dad.

At 17, heading back to London after family vacation in Costa Del Sol, Spain.

The Tempo racing dinghy I learned my lesson in.

With my dad, just before my July 1980 intake into the Air Force, at my mom's flat in Bramley, Johannesburg.

In fatigues at Valhalla Air Force base, with Mom , first visitors day, six weeks into basic training.

Same day, photo taken by my mom.

My final Uitklaar (Checkout) from the South African Air Force, with my sister Shelley.

Millionaires Club cabaret, with dancers (L-R) Adele, me and Laura.

Pas de Deux with Jenni Lyn at Ruby Tuesday, my last show before leaving for The Moulin Rouge.

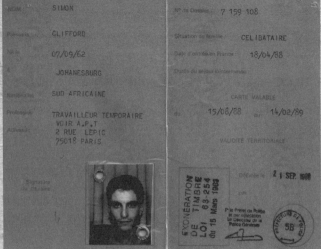

My one-year carte de séjour dated March 15, 1988, allowing me to work at The Moulin Rouge.

Standing on Rue Lepic dresse[d in]
typical 1980s attire: headban[d]
and leather necklace.

The double doors
of my apartment
on Rue Lepic,
my first Paris
apartment.

Entrance to the inner courtyard of my upscale apartment on Rue de la Victoire in Opera.

A typical high kick required of all Moulin dancers.

While still in the chorus, in my costume for the Arabian number with Karl, a great guy from Holland.

My buddies(L-R) Gavin Mills, Joachim Staaf and me, dressed in our Viennese waltz costumes.

(L-R) Joachim, Gavin and me in our principal Arabian costumes. Note the whip.

The famous white stallion MacBeth with Gavin, me and Joachim.

High kicks and high jinx on The Moulin Rouge stage. I'm on the far right, in perfect form of course.

Backstage waiting to go on for second part of Arabian sequence.

The guys and me hanging out in the principals' dressing room.

Relaxing. My right foot is bandaged, but the show must go on, February 1989, just before I became a principal.

Backstage with one
of the 180-pound
alligators.

Up close and
personal with
an African
python.

Madame Damaris Loubser
Attachée (Migration)
près l'Ambassade d'Afrique du Sud
a l'honneur d'inviter

Clif Simon + Guest

à un cocktail qui aura lieu le 2 Mars 1989
à l'ambassade à 18ʰ, au cours
duquel Melle Breytenbach présentera son
successeur, Mr Hewetson

Ambassade d'Afrique du Sud
59, Quai d'Orsay
75007 Paris

R.S.V.P.
45 55 92 37
Poste 2119

Avant 27/2/89

Invitation to the South African Embassy, at
59 Quai d'Orsay, on March 2, 1989.

Gavin, his Moulin dancer girlfriend Sally, and me at
Café Palmier after a grueling two shows.

Just arrived in Stockholm into the waiting arms of my ice queen, Asa.

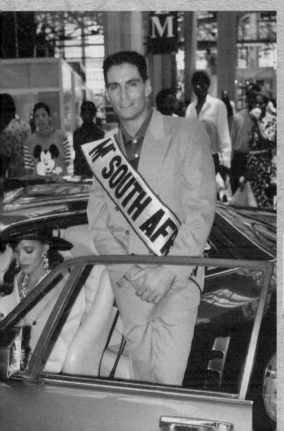

Winning the first Mr. South Africa competition in 1992.

DARE YOU IGNORE
THE NEW KIDS ON THE BLOCK

One of the print ads I did in a South African magazine, The ad reads, "Dirty Henry and Mad Max are Terrorizing the neighbourhood." Perfect.

DIRTY HENRY AND MAD MAX ARE TERRORIZING THE NEIGHBOURHOOD

Gracing the cover of *Keur* magazine, an Afrikaans publication, as Mitch Mitchell from the hugely successful daytime soap "Egoli: Place of Gold," February 25, 1994.

25 FEBRUARI

KEUR

R3,42

Geheime
liefdes
van Egoli se
Cliff Simon

So lyk die meisie
agter Liza se klavier

BONUS
Foto's van
rolprent

GRATIS: 3
verhale in
uithaalboek

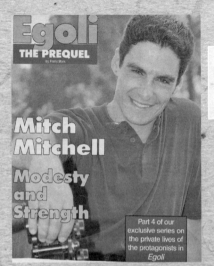

Egoli
THE PREQUEL
By Franz Marx

Mitch Mitchell

Modesty and Strength

Part 4 of our exclusive series on the private lives of the protagonists in *Egoli*

Cover of *Personality* magazine, 1995 as Mitch Mitchell, during my third season on the show.

This article featured me as 'Flying High-Mitch.' The article reads: "Colleagues say his modesty doesn't allow him to give himself enough credit for his rapid rise in the business world." Of course, I loved the helicopter.

Gregory (Mitch) Mitchell's usually smiling face was serious as he slipped almost furtively past his secretary's desk and into his office. "Please hold my calls," he instructed over his shoulder before closing the door behind him.

For a moment he considered locking the door, but he didn't. Surely his secretary wouldn't dream of allowing someone to enter after he had specifically asked her to hold his calls.

After a moment he walked across the plush sand-coloured carpet to the small safe against the opposite wall. Slowly he dialled the secret combination, opened the door and took out a thin leather folder.

This he carried back to the glass-and-chrome desk in front of the huge windows with their spectacular view of the city skyline. As he sat reading the familiar words, it was almost as if he could hear a voice from his past talking to him. He closed his eyes and sat back in his chair . . . remembering, thinking, considering.

He remained lost in thought until at last he reached a decision about his relationship with the beautiful Lynette Strydom. He closed the folder, locked it away and swung the office door wide open. "I think I will have that cup of coffee now, Sarah," he announced with a big smile . . .

Mitch Mitchell is what is known in marketing circles as a people's person — a warm and outgoing man who loves nothing more than being with people, talking to them, listening to them. "The last of the good guys," as one of his employees puts it. "The only boss I've ever had who actually listens to you," adds another.

But whenever he faces a major problem in life — personal or business — he withdraws from the outside world and goes through that same strange ritual involving the thin leather folder containing what he considers to be his most precious possession.

"It's just my way of focusing on

Flying high — Mitch's colleagues say his modesty doesn't allow him to give himself enough credit for his rapid rise in the business world.

Man on the move — Mitch hams it up for his marketing colleagues.

Some ancient words of wisdom from the East? Or perhaps a bank statement or a share certificate to remind him of the fact that he is one of the most successful young businessmen in Johannesburg? Or what about the fancy certificate he received last year when he was named Young Marketer of the Year?

"Nothing like that," he answers with another sheepish grin that makes him look much younger than his 36 years. "It's only a handwritten letter on cheap foolscap paper — the last I ever received from José de Capriles.

"He was a remarkable man, a strange combination of all sorts of things," is how Mitch describes the Brazilian business tycoon who started out being his boss and ended up becoming his friend and mentor. "He had the razor-sharp brain of a top international businessman, the heart of a typical Latin-American playboy — and the soul of a peasant.

"He always maintained that any of the simple workers on one of his coffee estates back in Brazil knew a lot more about life than a Harvard or Oxford-educated city slicker ever could. So when you went to him with a problem, chances were that he'd throw an old proverb back at you and leave you to figure out the solution from that piece of folk wisdom.

"He loved to quote what Mark Twain said about the difference between school and education: 'I've never let my schooling interfere with my education!'"

Even though José de Capriles has been dead for a few years, Mitch still uses his memories of the remarkable man whenever he's faced with a major problem in his life. "I take out the letter of advice he wrote to me before his death, reread it and

Big Screen magazine with me on the cover.

NEW ... THE MOST SCANDALOUS GOSSI

BIG SCREEN

THE MOVIE MAGAZIN

REELIN
We revie
truly awf
video

WHO THE #*!%# IS
Howard Stern?

THE FIFTH ELEMEN
The Biggest movie ever?

pull out & keep celebrity portfolio

featuring egoli's CLIFF SIMON • SEPUTLA SEBOGO
michelle constant • ASHLEY HAY • urban cree

Athena underwear television commercial shot in the Drakensberg Mountains. Itchy shot for sure, 1996.

The awesome Suzuki I bought from Gavin on my return from Paris. Mom always told me to never buy a motorbike.

Working at Casino Estoril in Portugal, 1991 with my beautiful lady Colette before we got married.

Engagement party.(L-R) My dad Mannie, me, my mom Phyllis and Colette, 1993.

Photo shoot of Colette and me on Guincho Beach in Portugal, the most spectacular beach, 1991.

Overhead lift with Colette, a stunning dancer. She always put me to shame.

Four years after getting engaged we got married at Bakubung Lodge on November 1, 1997. Entire wedding covered exclusively by *Sarie*, a life-style magazine.

Cliff trou met sy Colette

<23

deur die Johannesburgse bloemis Franz Gräbe word sy die rondawel eiegelewe en goud in koue water gedruk teen die warm son. Byna duidelik is die vertrek gevul met die soetste geure en ook wit blom donkbaar. Skielik is die bruid op die sefoon. Die video-man moes al 'n uur gelede hier gewees het ... Die senuwees begin so effe knaag. En waar is die troufotograaf?

ELDERS by Bakubung skarrel werkers tussen die verskillende plekke vir die troue - dit is immers "die geleentheid van die jaar", herinner die bestuurder, Luke Sacco.

Die markeastent onder by die seeboelpool (Bakubung beteken "mense van die seekoei") waar die huweliksplegtigheid gaan plaasvind, staan gereed en wit in die son. Tentpale word verskier met wit en takke groen en rooiese ryk. Stoele staan in rel/ese ryk.

'n Paar kilometer verder in die veld is die kos- en drankbestuurder, Paul Garratt, en sy

span besig om die Bakubungboma ("vergaderplek") te ontskep in 'n Afrika-paradys vir meer as honderd gaste. Die rooi tapyt word letterlik uitgerol!

Weerskante van die tapyt word gereed gemaak vir reusa-verwelkomingsware. Tafels word oorgetrek met spierwit tafeldoeke en gaste se sieraute staan kordaat in vergulde foto-raampies by elke sitplek. Franz Gräbe se bosse wit blomme en kerse toring hoog bo die tafels uit en hier en daar word gasiampies neergesit vir ekstra lig wanneer die son sak in die land van die groot vyf.

Berkant draai tien, koebe en twee reëlmatig op die spit en swaar yisterpotte word aangedra met vir paella en steurgarnale tot roomaartappels en sappige sampoene.

Bo in Luke Sacco se huis word 'n tafeltjie gereedgemaak vir die amptelike onderteke-ning van die huweliksregister. En in vir tuin maak ek en die fotograaf David Dodds haastig planne om 'n voorblaffoto vir

1. Twee Egoli-aktrises, Brümilda van Rensburg en Corien Pelt, wag om die bruid geluk te wens.

2. Peter Senskal en Darice Metzler was onder die gaste.

3. Die strooijonker, Jonny Leeb, en Julie Falcke.

4. Die Egoli-sterre Catriona Andrew (links) en Chantell Stander. In die middel is Chantell se man, Nick Rankin.

5. Axel Abrahamse, Monique Builache, Colin Bacon en die Egoli-aktrise Corine Pelt-Bacon.

6. Luke Sacco, bestuurder van Bakubung, by die paagetroudes.

7. 'n Franse croquembouche-troukoek wat die asem wegslaan.

8. Die troupaar klink 'n glasie.

9. Colette en Cliff geniet ontbyt op hul private balkon by Tshukudu, twintig minute se ry van Bakubung en in die hart van die Pilanesberg. Agter hulle is die uitgestrekte vlaktes waar die groot vyf gereeld vergader en besoekers 'n unieke blik gee op Afrika. Wildbewaarders, wat die omgewing haarfyn ken, neem besoekers daagliks op ritte en uitstappies. En die kos is uit 'n ander wêreld.

7. Colette en haar pa verlaat die Bazubung-rondawel minute voor die plegtigheid.
8. 'n Anderse troukar vir die bruid.
9. Ringe word uitgeruil.
10. Die marklestent waar meer as honderd gaste gewag het vir die 'troue van die jaar.'
11. Die amptelike huweliksregister word geteken.

Sarie magazine exclusive, me and my beautiful bride.

Saying our vows.

Colette and me after the ceremony.

(L-R) My mom Phyllis, me, my beautiful bride Colette and my dad.

After honeymooning in Switzerland, we hit Paris. Colette and I are standing outside The Lido.

Colette doing her thing outside The Moulin Rouge.

Our friend invited us to The Paradis Latin show.

As the evil Ba'al for seven seasons recurring in the hugely successful sci/fi series *Stargate SG1*.

My awesome bull terriers Montana and Harley on the beach in Malibu.

My boy, Harley and me on the beach. Montana was no longer with us.

Colette and me sailing in Santa Monica bay.

My best mate and great actor, Gideon, on a boat drooling at the LA Boat Show.

Got to fly the real Blackhawk flight simulator at Fort Rucker in Alabama.

Signing autographs for the soldiers at Fort Rucker, Alabama.

On set of *NCIS: New Orleans.*

Free to roam on my favorite toy.

On set, *Stargate SG1*, the infamous and arrogant Ba'al in *Continuum* the movie.

On set of *The Americans*. Honored to be working with the amazing Keri Russell and Mathew Rhys.

THE AMERICANS

"THE DEAL"

US: March 26, FX | UK: April 12, ITV

The Americans social media marketing.

My beautiful mix boxer pitbull Duma, meaning Cheetah in Swahili.

Chapter 10: Rebel Yell

The owl flies by night, a dark shadow passing through the darkness; he hoots his sinister quivering hoot as though he delights in the intoxicating black immensity of space.
Guy de Maupassant

A few months after I joined the Moulin Rouge, management threw a party. It was an opportunity to meet the cast – there were about one hundred people in "Formidable" and you only really get to know the people who are in a number with you. It's like shooting a film. You do your scene, and that's it. At the Moulin, someone could be in the show, and your paths would never cross, except during the finale.

The dressers, the front-of-stage management, the stunt men, the animal trainer, and all the dancers were invited to the party. The only person absent was the owner, Monsieur Clerico. He never fraternized with anyone. He left stage matters up to the choreographers and dance captains.

There was a lot of drinking, and joking around at the party. Things were going well with the show. I mingled for a polite amount of time, and then stepped away. I needed to be alone. I've always been that way even when I was a kid.

I took a bottle of wine and walked downstairs to the stage. The room was entirely dark. I sat in the middle of the stage drinking straight out of the bottle; muffled sounds of laughter and partying floated into the air from upstairs. I could still feel the heat from the stage lights, which had just been turned off, and the energy of the performers. The temperature would not come down for a couple of hours. I couldn't believe I was sitting on the stage of the Moulin Rouge in Paris. Truthfully, I never imagined that I would be good enough to be there.

I was getting very drunk. The wine bottle was almost empty. I looked out and could make out the tables and chairs. The linens had been removed; the waiters had done a cleanup and would be returning in the morning to vacuum the room. But I could still smell the cigarette smoke, and the odor of Champagne and liquor lingered in the air. The ghosts of all the dancers and singers from the day the Moulin first opened were in the walls. I felt as if the room and the heavy velvet curtains held their memories, and that someone was watching me, not in a threatening way, but as if to say "You are one of us now."

I felt privileged to be there on the heels of Billie Holiday, Edith Piaf, Maurice Chevalier, Yves Montand, and Frank Sinatra. I wished my parents would come to Paris and see me perform. I missed them, but I didn't miss Joburg. It paled in comparison to the vibrancy and freedom of Paris. There is a rhythm and pulse to the city, and nowhere did I feel it more acutely than performing on the stage of the Moulin Rouge with its electric energy.

In a few short months, Paris had become the center of my universe. I would eventually discover that Paris was, in reality, the center of everything that was happening throughout Europe in the 1980s. It was the center of fashion, the center of drug trafficking, the center of prostitution, and the center of money laundering. And whatever happened in Paris, reverberated throughout Europe. As German Prince Metternich wrote, "When Paris sneezes, Europe catches a cold."

That night, I felt as if my life had kicked into high gear:

that I had direction and purpose, which I could commit to with passion and confidence. I now had a career. If I wanted to stay at the Moulin Rouge for the rest of my life, I could have – if not as a dancer, eventually in management.

* * * *

Parisians don't celebrate Halloween, but the cabaret community – because there are so many expats – threw a big party and dance competition in the downstairs warehouse of the Lido de Paris on the Champs-Élysées across from the posh Georges V Hotel. Every dancer from the big shows in Paris was invited: the Crazy Horse, the Paradis Latin, the Lido, and the Moulin Rouge. As part of the festivities, there was a friendly dance competition; each club was asked to organize a special number for the party. It was a "dance off."

Gavin Mills was appointed the choreographer for the Moulin Rouge number. He chose Billy Idol's "Rebel Yell" for our music. I was dressed as a Rambo character in a torn tank top with fake blood all over my face and body. Gavin wore Arabian-style pants. I had a bottle of whiskey while waiting for our turn on stage and I kept drinking. As we got in position on the revolving stage, I still had the bottle with me. I said to Gavin, "Watch what I do in this number." He knew this meant trouble, but he didn't know what I was planning.

There was a line of judges sitting on folding chairs in front of the stage. The other dancers who would be competing and those who had just come to watch were screaming and cheering as each troupe took its position.

As I was dancing, I took the bottle and threw it down right in front of the judges for effect. It exploded, and the judges had a look on their faces like, "What the hell is going on?" but Gavin and I had a reputation as bad boys, so they weren't really surprised. Then the stage turned, and the Bluebell Girls and the Lido Boy Dancers were in position for their number.

The energy in the room was unbelievable. All of us had already done our regular shows, so we were running on sheer adrenaline. With a lot of fanfare, the judges announced the winner: "Paradis Latin." It was no surprise because their company had the most highly-trained ballet dancers; the rest of us were good dancers and gymnasts and put on a great show, but we didn't have their technical skills, and that was what the judges were looking for, not an exploding whiskey bottle thrown at their feet.

By the time the party ended, it was nearly dawn, and everyone was completely wasted from too much alcohol. We were like vampires – living for the night and sleeping during the day when the sun was at its zenith.

I was dating a British dancer with the Nouvelle Eve Theater a couple of blocks south of the Moulin Rouge. Caroline and I left the party with Gavin and Sally, his live-in girlfriend, and our friend from South Africa, Luiz, who was working at the same theater as Caroline. We were still wearing our costumes from the dance competition. I was holding another bottle of whiskey, and Caroline was carrying a small television set, which she had won in a raffle at the party. The fresh October air hit our faces as we swaggered down the street. The dawn light was pushing the last vestiges of darkness away, but a fading moon still hung in the Paris sky.

Gavin decided he needed to take a pee, so he hauled it out

right in the middle of the Champs-Élysées. There were people on their way to work, so he caused quite a commotion, and the *gendarmes* were called. I heard sirens blaring, and then the cops jumped out and put us in their van. When they saw the television set, they thought we had stolen it. We were all pretty drunk, and I was still covered in dried, fake blood.

The police couldn't figure out if we were hard-core criminals or just a troupe of ruffians, but they weren't about to take any chances. When we got into the van, a short policeman addressed our motley gang, "Sit down right now." I refused.

Gavin pleaded with me, "Cliff, just sit down."

"I don't want to sit down. What's he going to do?" Gavin threw me a look, and repeated himself, but I wouldn't budge. I wanted to use my height to intimidate the cop.

I stayed on my feet. The cop turned on his walkie-talkie to alert the station that he was on his way, and said he might be bringing trouble with a capital T.

It was about a ten-minute ride to the police station. The cops opened up the back of the van and told us to line up. I started screaming in English, "Fuck you. Fuck you. I'm not lining up. Who do you think you are?" The cop pushed me into line.

"Gavin, tell that fucker not to push me. If he tries that again, I'm going to clock him, I swear." All of a sudden memories of being in the Air Force in South Africa flooded over me, and I reacted. It was as if Flight Sergeant Dick Head was grinding his boot against the back of my head.

Gavin told the police that we would agree to go inside the station, but we were not marching in a line. Once we were inside, Caroline announced that she needed to go to the bathroom. She asked the cop to show her to the ladies room. He led her down the hallway and then opened the door to his office. "The bathroom is in here." Gavin translated for me, and I got up from the bench. I started running for the cop. I was going to grab him. Gavin jumped up and dived on me. I was screaming, "Don't you dare lay a hand on my girlfriend. I am going to fuckin' kill you." At that point, I meant it. If it wasn't for Gavin, I would have attacked the cop and probably would have ended up in jail for assault on a police officer. I would have been fired from the Moulin, and it would have been the end of my time in Paris. Gavin saved my skin. I came very close to being in a lot of trouble.

Gavin kept insisting to the police, "We are Moulin Rouge dancers." Usually, that was enough to get them off our backs, but it wasn't. While the Préfecture de Police and the Moulin had a very cordial relationship when it came to work permits and the like, if dancers stepped out of line and made trouble, they were on their own. At the time, Gavin and I were naïve enough to think that we could pull any prank we wanted to and get away with it. This was not the case, as we discovered.

Since it was so early in the morning, we had to wait almost two hours for the police to reach the Moulin Rouge production office to verify our identities. The *gendarmes* eventually let us go, but not before having a good time messing around with us.

* * * *

Gavin liked to organize a boys' night out. Whenever we could, we'd take the same night off so that we could go gallivanting around Paris together without Gavin's live-in girlfriend, Sally. I was dating a lot of different girls, so I had no one to worry about. I could do what I wanted. At twenty-six, I didn't want to make a commitment to anyone, and I wasn't interested in a long-term relationship. Frankly, what was usually on my mind was sex with no strings attached. It would be several years before I was mature enough to find true love with someone to whom I could freely commit myself.

There are a number of very elegant nightclubs in Paris, and Gavin and I used to drift from one to the next, getting drunker by the hour. On one particular night, he suggested Le Palace, a trendy club known for its loud electronic house music, which attracted a mix of sophisticated Parisians and expats. Le Palace was housed in an ornate, gilded theater on Rue du Faubourg-Montmartre. There was a downstairs bar and a huge dance floor with a DJ spinning British and American records. The upstairs balconies – where theatergoers used to sit – had cocktail tables and a second, much larger bar. The original building dated back to the seventeenth century and had survived the French Revolution and Baron Haussmann's modernization of Paris. For many years, it was used as a dance hall. It was then converted into a nightclub and became one of the Parisian nightlife hot spots in the late 1970's.

A bouncer dressed in a dark business suit stood guard at the front door of Le Palace to keep the riff raff out. The dance floor was packed and "The Only Way Is Up," by Yazz and the Plastic Population, was blasting over the loudspeakers when we sauntered in. Gavin gave the bouncer his jacket, but I kept mine on. We ordered straight tequila at the downstairs bar. I said to Gavin, "I'm going to walk around upstairs." Then I added, "Please, don't start any trouble." When he was not with Sally, he sometimes went wild, and from the look in his eyes, I was sure that this was going to be one of those crazy nights.

I stood at the balcony, watching couples dancing downstairs to Depeche Mode's "Just Can't Get Enough." I looked around to see if there was a pretty girl to flirt with, but no one caught my eye. In less than fifteen minutes, I heard a commotion downstairs over the blare of music. Two black bouncers were muscling their way through the crowd with a guy being dragged by his arms between them. I looked over the balcony, and of course, it was Gavin. I took the stairs, two at a time. Gavin's shirt was already off. I don't know if he took it off or if it was ripped off, but the effect on the crowd was the same. They were highly entertained.

Gavin was swearing at the bouncers. This time, it was my turn to be the voice of reason, and get my buddy out of a mess. I told the bouncers, "Let him go. I'm his friend. I'll take care of him." I thought I might save the day, but Gavin was wound up. He said to me, "Let's fuckin' fight them."

"Are you crazy? We're drunk. Look at the size of these guys. They'll kill us."

The bouncers escorted us to the door, and Gavin turned around yelling, "My jacket. I need my jacket." They retrieved his jacket and then stood shoulder to shoulder to make sure we weren't thinking about coming back to cause more trouble. I felt relieved – disaster averted, or so I thought.

Next door to Le Palace was a hot dog stand. Patrons were perched on stools outside enjoying their food. Gavin started shouting in English to no one in particular, "I hate the French.

Fuck you all," as he walked toward the hot dog stand. We passed by, and then Gavin turned around and smacked a guy right off his stool on to the sidewalk. .The poor guy hit the deck like a sack of potatoes. Gavin continued ranting. I grabbed him as the guy started to pick himself up off the pavement. He charged toward all 6'3 of Gavin. That takes balls. I could have protected him, but I thought, *You know what? I'm going to let him take a swing at Gavin*, and he did, right in the gut. He deserved what he got.

I apologized for Gavin and shoved him into his Mini Cooper, Oliver. Gavin was in no shape to be driving, so I got behind the wheel and drove us back to his apartment on Rue de La Madone. Gavin was still ranting and raving. Sally was waiting for us and took Gavin into the bedroom and tried to calm him down. I was standing in the living room. I could hear Gavin yelling at her, "I don't want to be with you. I want to be with Cliff." She came out of the bedroom and asked me, "What's going on? He's spitting at me. How much did he have to drink? He stinks, and he's drenched in sweat."

"I know. Just take care of him. You know how crazy he gets."

She did know, and she put up with it for a few years, until they eventually parted after Sally got tired of Gavin's benders, and Gavin was ready to settle down with someone else. (In 1992 Gavin and I worked at the first Miss World competition held at Sun City, South Africa, where Gavin met Miss Hungary, Bernadett Papp. (Who later became his wife.)

Gavin was very charismatic, and he was always fun to be around, especially when something set him off. He spoke

French well enough, so I was willing to let him be the initiator, and I was his first lieutenant. Sometimes, when he got into a fight, he'd look around for me, and expect me to step in. We were like Two Musketeers, and our friend Luiz was the third. Joachim didn't party with us to much because he was loyal to his French girlfriend Sandrine, who worked at the Moulin.

Gavin and I had a lot in common. We had both served in the military in South Africa, and with that kind of training, we never backed away from a good fight. In fact, while we were in Paris we could have been accused of starting one or two brawls.

Gavin's idea of an exciting night in Paris was to drive down the Champs-Élysées at full speed to the Arc de Triomphe, and stop his car in the middle of the roundabout in the thick of evening traffic. Twelve streets feed into the Place Charles de Gaulle. At the center is the Arc de Triomphe with the names of the various battles fought and won by France engraved into the stone and underneath is the Tomb of the Unknown Soldier. Gavin would stand next to his car just to hear all the French shouting at him and honking their horns. He was a real provocateur. He'd shout back at the drivers for ten or fifteen minutes before he had his fill of fun and mayhem. The police never stopped him, and he pulled this prank regularly. I used to sit in the passenger seat of Oliver, watching his antics with a mixture of amusement and dread. I think the French had started getting on Gavin's nerves, and he must have thought, *What better place to send out a "Fuck You" than the Arc de Triomphe*, which was the patriotic epicenter of Paris.

Despite our history of brawls and crazy antics, Gavin and

I did know how to behave properly when it was absolutely necessary. We were invited to a party at the South African embassy in Paris by Madame Damaris Loubser, the cultural attaché. It was the first time that there were two male dancers from South Africa performing at the Moulin Rouge, so we were celebrities among the South African expat community, and I am sure she thought it would be amusing to have us on the guest list.

The embassy was on the Ile de la Cité on the tree-lined Quai d'Orsay at number 59 in the seventh arrondissement. It was *l'heure bleue* when it is neither daylight nor darkness, what poets call the sweet light when dusk settles over Paris before the streetlights are turned on and monuments are illuminated to show off their splendor.

Gavin and I arrived at the reception wearing our best suits because we were representing the Moulin Rouge. As we entered the mansion, we saw huge antique vases filled with flowers and bronze statues of various mythological characters. The reception room was wood paneled and reminded me of an old hunting lodge built by British colonialists. Foreign ambassadors and multi-millionaires were grazing on *pâté de foie gras* and drinking Veuve Clicquot or dry martinis. There was a musical interlude – a pianist and a singer performing *lieder* from the Schumann repertoire, I think. Despite all the dignitaries, Gavin and I were probably the most sought-after men in the room. We stood out from the rest of the crowd, and some of the guests were curious to hear what it was like to work at the famous Moulin Rouge. Our behind-the-scenes tales were far more fascinating to them than the fluctuation of the *krugerand* against the franc.

Madame Loubser was charming and very beautiful. The de Klerk government made an excellent choice in dispatching her to work at the South African embassy in Paris because Frenchmen always enjoy doing business with an attractive, intelligent woman. They are more likely to accept an invitation to dinner with her than with a male diplomat. At the time, relations between South Africa and France were cordial. Not wanting to antagonize South Africa, France kept its nose out of the apartheid business. (Its own history of black exploitation in the former French West African colonies was well-known.)

South Africa was an important customer of the French-made Mirage jet fighter plane, and France wanted to keep the money flowing into its coffers. The French were also more interested in buying South Africa's diamonds and gold than speaking out against apartheid.

I suspect that the embassy and its attaché, Madame Damaris Loubser, kept a watchful eye on the legitimate buying and selling of jets, gold, and diamonds. I would soon find myself in the middle of "South African-French trade relations," in a manner that could have ended my life or landed me in jail for a very long time.

Chapter 11: Vigilantes

Attack is the secret of defense. Defense is the planning of attack.

Sun Tzu, *The Art of War*

When Baron Haussmann modernized Paris and cleared away its slums in the late nineteenth century, he made sure to design sidewalks large enough to accommodate chairs and tables so that the city's bistros and cafés could enhance their seating capacity and satisfy the Parisian urge to see and be seen.

With the first crocuses pushing through the ground in the springtime, chairs and tables are set up outside and from early morning, there is a busy street scene where Parisians can sit for hours perusing *Le Monde* or the *International Herald Tribune* while sipping imported coffee from Africa. At closing time well past midnight, the waiters stack the chairs and tables, chaining everything together to protect them against thieves until the next morning, when the cycle begins anew until the weather turns cold in November, and then everyone moves indoors until spring returns.

Patrons at Le Palmier sitting at the sidewalk tables had a direct view of the Moulin Rouge across the Place Blanche. The grating over the Métro was a gathering place for Moulin dancers who stood around for a quick smoke and a chat between numbers, unrecognized by the café habitués. In front of the café was one of the few remaining *pissoirs*, which was notorious for clandestine trysts and drug deals. The café patrons sitting outside needed to keep their eyes open for thieves who operated throughout Pigalle, especially during the warm summer months.

It was a glorious summer evening in mid-July, four months after I arrived in Paris. I was still in the chorus, but I was already notorious among the dancers and management at the Moulin Rouge for my high jinx and aggressive behavior, especially with Gavin by my side. We quickly earned a reputation as vigilantes among the denizen of Pigalle.

Some of the Moulin Rouge dancers were enjoying drinks at Le Palmier (Now named, Rouge Ibis) after the second show. Gavin and I were inside playing a video game. Chantal Ortolan stopped at our table before making her next score of the evening. She bragged to Gavin that she had just landed a big fish – a Brit on holiday – and business was picking up for her. All the while chatting with Gavin, she flirted with me. She put her hand on my shoulder and in perfect English, said, "So good to see you again, Cleef. Catch you later," and she was off.

"I don't like her."

Gavin said, "Oh, she's just having fun with you. She might even have a crush on you. She used to come on to me until I settled in with Sally."

I ordered a whiskey.

Suddenly, I heard one of the girls scream, "He's got my bag. He's got my bag." I ran outside and saw an Arab-looking guy holding a big bag pushing his way through the dancers who were hanging out on the street. The girl continued screaming, "He stole my bag." Without thinking, I took off. The thief saw me coming after him and sprinted down Boulevard de Clichy.

My first thought was, *Why the hell am I wearing cowboy boots*? They were slowing me down, but I sprinted and caught up with him. As I dived for him, a car coming in the opposite direction headed right for us. He cushioned the blow as the car hit us, I felt his body crunch. Then, as if in automatic mode I felt my fists pummeling his face. The police arrived, pulled me off him, and put him in their car. The police were already out looking for him, which explains why they showed up on the scene so quickly.

I walked back to Le Palmier carrying the bag. My knees and elbows were bleeding. Everyone started clapping and yelling Bravo. I sat down to catch my breath and took a gulp of my drink. Gavin got up and left. But that is not the end of the story. The next minute someone yelled, "Gavin's in a fight." I put my drink down thinking, *Here we go again.*

I ran outside again and across the street from Le Palmier was Monsieur Henri, who is the long-time manager of the restaurant at the Moulin Rouge, with Gavin and Sally. Three guys had them surrounded. Arms were flailing about. Gavin was trying to protect Monsieur Henri, but one of the guys jumped on Gavin's back. I grabbed the guy from behind and picked him up over my head and threw him into the street. I was a lot bigger, stronger and taller than he was. As he was lying in the street, he pulled out a knife. I felt my blood boil. I yelled at him, "That's the last thing you want to do." He didn't know it, but I had grown up in a gun culture, and a knife didn't scare me. In fact, it made me angrier. He tried to stand up, and I laid into him, slamming him on the ground again and disarming him.

Another fight started. I think Gavin was in the middle of it, but I didn't have time to look around because I was holding the guy down waiting for the cops. And then there was the sound of police sirens. A *flic* grabbed one of my arms when I laid into the guy on the ground. The policeman tried to pull me off the guy, but I wanted to finish him off. Then the man who ran the pizza joint on the Place Blanche showed up; he grabbed me by my other arm and shouted, "Just let go of the *flic's* arm. It's finished." The police saw the pizza man and let go of me. I walked back to Le Palmier. I didn't want to have anything more to do with the police. The cops followed us into Le Palmier, and told Gavin and me, "You need to come to the police station to identify these thugs and make a statement."

I said, "Gavin, you go. I'm not going to any police station," because I was afraid of what I might do or say. The guy had pulled a knife on me, and if I saw him again, I wanted to bash his head in for threatening me.

Gavin cooperated with the police. When he got back from the station, he said, "Dude, they just arrested eleven gang members. These guys are all from Morocco. They come into Paris during the summertime, work the streets and then go back with as much loot as they can steal."

He continued, "After I gave my deposition and identified the three guys, they were threatening me, yelling from their jail cells, 'We're going to get you. We're going to kill you. You're dead meat.'"

I thought it was the usual rubbish, but Gavin was visibly shaken. The cops told him, "Don't worry. These guys are out of here. We're going to deport them. They'll never get back into France. Period. End of story."

Monsieur Henri was very grateful to Gavin and me for rescuing him. He said, "You're my boys." The Moulin Rouge had never seen two tall, strong former military guys from South Africa ready and willing to take on the riff raff of Paris. We both assured management that if anyone at the Moulin needed our protection, we were available. We were definitely in their good graces, but I didn't know that this story had gone up the chain of command from Monsieur Henri to the owner of the Moulin Rouge, Monsieur Jacki Clerico.

* * * *

A few nights later, I was finishing the "Viennese Waltz" number during the second show. From the stage, I spotted a stunning girl sitting in the front row. The stage lights spilled over her blond hair. She smiled at me, and I smiled back at her. I ran off stage, changed into my next costume, and wrote her a quick note inviting her to meet me at the stage door after the show. I rolled the note up, and when I went back out on stage, I flicked it at her. Unfortunately, it hit the guy sitting next to her and rolled off the table. He picked it up and read it. I thought, *Does he think I want to meet him?* I waited for him to look up and when he did, I pointed at the girl sitting next to him. He understood. She read my note and smiled at me again. I ran to the stage door and held it open looking for her. (Does this sound familiar? It was.) Everyone was piling out of the Moulin Rouge. She managed to push her way through the crowd. I waved at her to come to the door. She barely spoke any English, but in a mixture of English and Italian, she explained that she was an Italian guide and that the people with her were on a tour of Paris. I asked her if she'd take a coffee with me.

"*Mi dispiace.* I'm sorry. I must take my people back to our hotel."

"I can meet you there later. Where are you staying?"

She wrote down the name of her hotel. I went up to her room, and we had a fantastic night. It was the start of a fine romance. Every week during the summer she brought an Italian tour group to Paris, and we'd spend at least one night together.

Sophia was utterly charming, with a sparkling personality. One evening, I took her for a drink at Le Palmier with Gavin and Sally. As usual, the café was filled with Moulin Rouge dancers and customers from all over the world.

When we walked into the café together, Chantal Ortolan was sitting in a corner with another prostitute. Chantal looked at me with a nasty sneer on her face. I told Sophia, "Hold on a minute. I'm going over to see what her problem is with me." Chantal started swearing at me, picked up a glass of wine, threw it in my face, and then stormed out of the café.

I was completely blind-sided. I told her friend, who was also dark-skinned and from Morocco, "I have no idea what's going on here. Why the hell did she do that? I have always been polite to her. " I knew that Chantal was part of a prostitution ring and had protection. I certainly didn't want to get into an altercation with her.

"Cleef, Chantal is in love with you, and she is very jealous you are with that Italian, blond girl all the time."

"I haven't given Chantal Ortolan any reason to think I'm interested in her. *Au contraire.*"

"Eh, *bien.* The heart wants what it wants."

I went back to our table. Sophia and I finished our drinks and walked back with Gavin and Sally to his car, which was parked in front of the Moulin Rouge. Chantal came running at me across Place Blanche through the late-night traffic, screaming at me in French. I didn't understand what she was saying but from the look on her face, it could only mean trouble. I opened the car door and told Sophia to get in right away. Chantal ran up to me and started yanking my leather necklace, trying to pull it off. I said, "Get off of me," but she wouldn't stop and the necklace didn't break. I didn't want to touch her. I signaled to Gavin to help me, but he just held up his hands as if to say, "I'm not getting involved in this." It was too dangerous, even for him.

I don't hit women, ever, and I despise men who do, but I had to get her off me. I backhanded her, and she crumpled onto the pavement. She looked at me with fire in her eyes and said, "This isn't finished. This isn't finished." I thought, *Shit, I just hit a streetwalker. This could be bad.*

Gavin and Sally dropped us off at Sophia's hotel. I spent what was left of the night with her. As usual, it was fantastic. I tried never to let anything get in the way of sexual pleasure, but in the back of my mind I knew that word would get out on the street, and if it did that would spell trouble for me. No doubt about it. Chantal Ortolan was a valuable commodity, and I had just hit her. I felt sick.

At dawn, I took the Métro back from Sophia's hotel to my apartment on Rue de la Victoire. The night before, somebody had taken my spot in the courtyard, so I left my car on the street. I fell into bed exhausted from a night of lovemaking and slept fitfully. When I got up at about noon, I took a quick shower, made myself a cup of coffee, and then opened the heavy doors of the courtyard out on to Rue de la Victoire. My car was parked where I had left it the previous evening, but there was a bouquet of dead red roses tucked under the windshield wipers. I had seen enough murder mysteries and read enough spy thrillers to know that this was bad. Chantal or one of her goons had followed me back to my apartment from Sophia's hotel, and now they knew where I lived.

I ran back upstairs to look for a weapon. I got a kitchen knife and stuck it inside one of the leather boots I was wearing, and I put a stick inside my jacket sleeve. I thought about taking my car to the Moulin, but I decided I'd rather walk. Someone might have put a pipe bomb underneath my car. My imagination was getting the better of me, but I didn't want to take any chances. I had seen worse things than that in South Africa – ANC vigilantes setting fire to cars, kidnapping whites from their houses, planting bombs in trash cans.

It was eight o'clock in the evening. I found Monsieur Thierry, who was talking to one of the chorus boys. I needed to speak with him immediately. I told him about the fight with Chantal, and finding the dead flowers on my car. He winced, "*Les Fleurs du Mal.*"

"What do you mean?"

"*The Flowers of Evil.* It's a poem by Baudelaire. Read it someday."

I was in no mood for a lesson in French literature. "I need to speak with Monsieur Clerico. Can you arrange it? This is serious."

Thierry gave me his standard response. "Monsieur Clerico doesn't make appointments with the cast. He leaves these matters up to Doris, Ruggero and me."

I asked him, "You want to mess with the Mob? I think they are somehow involved in this."

"All right. Come by tomorrow before the show. I'll talk to Monsieur Clerico. Maybe he'll see you."

For the first time since I had been in Paris, I felt nervous that something might happen to me. I had a feeling that I might need protection on the street, and who better to give it to me than Monsieur Clerico.

* * * *

I hadn't met Monsieur Jacki Clerico before. I had only seen publicity shots of him with the many stars who had performed at the Moulin Rouge. He had steel gray hair combed back, and perfectly tailored suits with expensive looking silk ties. The Moulin had been in the Clerico family since the 1950s, and he was credited with putting the venerable cabaret back on to a strong financial footing.

Monsieur Clerico carried himself like an upper-class gentleman. He was suave and debonair. The same words could have applied to my father: impeccably dressed, known for his good manners and charm – one a Lithuanian and the other from Piedmont on the border of France and Italy. Many of the front-of-house staff modeled their attire after Monsieur Clerico, wearing elegant tailor-made suits, and combing their hair back off their foreheads in a very regal and patrician manner. He drove a discrete dark blue Ferrari, as he was a huge fan of high-performance vehicles. He never parked the

Ferrari in front of the Moulin for show. I heard that he was a racehorse breeder, which explains why members of the British royal family, who were also horse lovers, attended Moulin premieres, along with special performances for Princess Diana and the Queen herself.

I walked upstairs into the offices of the Moulin for my meeting with Monsieur Clerico. All the walls are carpeted. There is no handle on the door into his office. You have to be buzzed in from the inside. Someone is watching you through a television camera, which was installed in such a way that the lobby is under surveillance at all times.

Monsieur Clerico was sitting behind a large mahogany desk smoking a cigar. We were alone. He was very soft spoken and greeted me in perfectly correct English. "Well, Cleef, tell me what's going on." When he stood up, I was surprised that he was not taller. His reputation suggested a man of stature, but he was short – at least compared to me.

I explained to him what had happened – the fight with Chantal Ortolan, the flowers and so forth. I said, "Look I'm just a performer. I am not looking for problems here. I am afraid that my car might be rigged with explosives. Someone knows where I live."

"In the Seventh? Near the Galeries Lafayette?"

I was surprised that he knew anything about me. I nodded.

He said, "Don't worry. Nothing is going to happen to you."

I thanked him for his time and left. I suspected that he had heard about what Gavin and I had done for the restaurant manager, Monsieur Henri, and this was a gesture of appreciation for his two South African vigilantes. If it hadn't been for that incident, I am not sure he would have even have agreed to a meeting, despite the fact that I was at this point a valuable member of the company.

What happened next was not anything I could tell Monsieur Clerico about. It was more sinister than Baudelaire's *Flowers of Evil*.

Chapter 12: Diamonds

There are three things extremely hard: steel, a diamond, and to know one's self.
Benjamin Franklin, U.S. Ambassador to France (1776-1785)

A week after my private meeting with Monsieur Clerico, the owner of the Moulin Rouge, I finished the second show and headed for Le Palmier. Crossing the Place Blanche, I looked over my shoulder to make sure that Chantal Ortolan or one of her bodyguards was not following me. I noticed a stranger sitting at an inside table at the café with a group of the dancers. He was tall with broad shoulders, dressed in an elegant business suit. He was engaged in friendly banter with the company. I walked over to his table, and one of the dancers introduced us. From that night, Jean-Paul latched on to me. (He never told me his last name. I think it might have been Caboche.) I remember thinking at the time, *Why is he getting so friendly with me? What does he want?* He also took a passing interest in Gavin, but not in the way he zeroed in on me.

Jean-Paul used to show up at Le Palmier every few days. One evening I was sitting next to him. He had his back to the wall and kept glancing out the front window. He didn't like sitting at one of the outside tables. Looking back on it, I think it might have made him feel too exposed. We had a good view of the cars parked across from the café. I saw a guy checking out a car, and one of the girls from the Moulin was leaning over the car. It looked a bit odd.

I said, "What's going on out there?"

"I just gave the girl the keys to my Porsche to get something out of the trunk."

Then someone else started fiddling with the door handle of the Porsche. Jean-Paul bolted out of his chair, ran across the street and grabbed him. He started shouting, hitting the guy, and in less than a minute, the guy ran off. I saw Jean-Paul open the trunk of his car; he took something out and then walked back to Le Palmier. Sitting back down next to me, he was hardly out of breath. I waited a few minutes, not saying anything. He was acting nuts, fidgeting with his car keys, his eyes darting around the café. He gulped down the glass of wine he had left on the table. Then he muttered, "Nobody can touch my fuckin' car." I had never heard him speak in such an uncouth manner. Until that moment, Jean-Paul had always presented himself as a real gentleman – calm, cool and collected. But I didn't blame him for becoming unnerved. I was the same way. When someone touches anything that belongs to me without my permission, I can go off – especially if it's my car.

A week later, Jean-Paul signaled me over to his table at Le Palmier. It was about two o'clock in the morning; the ashtray in front of him was full of cigarettes, and he had already had a couple of drinks. He said, "Do you want to come out with me, Cleef? I want to take you somewhere special."

I sat in the passenger seat of his metallic brown Porsche 930 Turbo. The interior was beautiful cream-colored leather, all hand-stitched. We drove into a neighborhood near the Arc de Triomphe. Parking in front of a club, there were a couple of older men standing outside. Jean-Paul led me to the front door. There was a red rope in front of the door, which was locked, but there was a glass portal so that someone on the other side could see who wanted to enter. The door opened. A man in a tuxedo exclaimed, "Ah, Monsieur Caboche. *Bonsoir*."

Gray-haired men were sitting on banquettes, drinking, and smoking, and there were gorgeous young girls on the dance floor. The waiter showed us to a table, and within seconds, and without a word from Jean-Paul, whiskey bottles were brought to the table. The waiter knew exactly what Jean-Paul wanted. It was obvious that he was a regular at the club. Over loud music, he pointed to the dance floor. "Nice girls. Which one do you want?" I surveyed the dance floor. "Those two look pretty cool." Jean-Paul tapped someone on the shoulder and instructed him to invite the girls over to our table. They didn't hesitate and slid onto the banquette. We poured drinks and finished off three bottles of whiskey in less than two hours. By this time, I was feeling light headed.

Jean-Paul announced in English, "Come on. Let's take these girls home with us."

I said, "I'm in, but where do you want to go?"

"To your apartment." I thought that was strange. I wondered, W*hy don't we go to your place?* But I didn't say anything. I suspected that he must have had his reasons, and I knew that he wasn't about to explain himself. Not then, anyway.

He squashed the girls into the pony seat in the back of the Porsche. The girls were laughing and carrying on. To them, this was all a big adventure, and they were at the club to pick up rich guys. They probably thought they had made a big score. Both girls were in their early twenties, dressed in revealing outfits.

I cranked the window open; the early morning summertime air felt refreshing and cleared my head. Jean-Paul drove fast. We arrived at Rue de la Victoire. I opened the heavy wooden doors into the courtyard, and we climbed two flights of stairs to my apartment. With each step, I asked myself, *Why does Jean-Paul want to come to my place? Does he want to know where I live? Does he want to see how I live? And if so, why?* I was beginning to feel paranoid, but I had enough confidence in myself to figure a way out if I fell into a trap. Two years in the South African military taught me how to take care of myself.

My studio apartment had a bed and a huge sofa which pulled out into a second bed. I fell into my bed with one girl, and Jean-Paul went at it with the other girl on the sofa. We were all laughing and checking one another out. None of us got any sleep. At about five o'clock in the morning, Jean-Paul announced, "Okay girls, why don't you just fuck off?"

I was shocked at the way he was speaking to them. I said, "Jean-Paul, I'm a gentleman. We should at least take them home."

"No. I just want them to fuck off."

The girls asked us to call them a taxi. He repeated himself. "No just fuck off. Get home on your own." They got dressed and left the apartment. I was cringing, and feeling very sorry for them. Jean-Paul was acting like a pig, but I was curious to see what he would do next. I have to admit that I was both attracted and repelled by his crass behavior.

"Cleef, let's go downstairs and get some steaks." There was a butcher shop next door, which was already open for business. The butcher knew me so he picked out two beautiful filets mignon. Jean-Paul prepared them for us on my two-burner stovetop; we ate, and then he left. I sat looking out my window at the pink, morning sky thinking that this had been a very surreal night. I had an inkling that stranger things were about to happen between Jean-Paul and me.

* * * *

"Cleef, I want to take you somewhere tonight." I thought *Jesus Christ, here we go again*, but I was up for another escapade despite having just done two shows at the Moulin Rouge. We drove to the Rue de Rivoli near the Place de la Concorde. Jean-Paul parked next to the colonnade. We downed a few tequilas quickly at a crowded bistro. I was feeling drunk from the booze and a bit fatigued. During the first show, one of the inexperienced chorus boys had gotten in my way, and I had fallen off the stage – the second time this had happened – and my arms and legs were pretty badly bruised.

We got back into the Porsche. Jean-Paul gunned the engine, and the Turbo hissed as it picked up speed. The street lights looked like streaks of tensile wires. The tires made a thumping sound as they hit the cobblestones. I caught a glimpse of the gilded statue of Joan of Arc astride her prancing horse, carrying a waving flag as if to urge us on to some unknown destination or into battle.

We should have been arrested, but there were no police cars around at that hour. We hit the open road at about 150 miles an hour. The tall trees created a natural arch over the road, and it was pitch black, the lights of Paris fading behind us. I had no idea where we were going. We were traveling too fast for me to read the blue and white road signs. Jean-Paul kept his attention on the road. He didn't want to break his concentration by talking to me. Or he didn't want to. We drove in silence for forty-five minutes. I calculated that we were about one hundred miles outside Paris by this time. And I had no way of getting back to Paris.

I could only see as far as the headlight beams. We seemed to be in the middle of the French countryside. Jean-Paul swerved off the road and drove down a gravel driveway. In front of us was a huge stone wall with a wooden gate. He honked his horn a couple of times; a slot in the wooden gate slid open, and a guard peered out at us. Then the gates swung open revealing a magnificent chateau with a parapet and manicured lawn. In the center was a marble fountain with a wood nymph holding an urn. Ferraris, Mercedes, and Rolls Royces were parked in the driveway. Most of the license plates ended in 75, indicating the owners were from central Paris. My car, a second-hand Fiat Ritmo, which I bought from one of the Nicolodi Brothers, would have looked very out of place here. But Jean-Paul's Porsche fit right in.

I followed Jean-Paul into the chateau. There was music playing, a dance floor, and waiters passing food among the well-dressed guests. It looked like a very exclusive, private club. Jean-Paul snapped his fingers, and a waiter ran over to him.

He turned to me. "Cleef, what do you want to eat?"

"A hamburger." He gave the waiter my order and told me to wait for him. Then he disappeared upstairs. I had a drink. No one approached me, and since I hardly spoke any French and had no idea who anyone was, I just looked around wondering what would happen next and was I going to have to bolt into the darkness.

This was the second time Jean-Paul had taken me to a members-only club. I couldn't figure out what message he was trying to send me, or what he wanted from me, but I was intrigued.

After an hour, Jean-Paul came downstairs carrying a briefcase. "Let's go."

"But I haven't finished my drink."

He jerked the drink out of my hand and downed what remained in the glass. "Let's go." I knew not to ask him what was in the briefcase, or what had gone on upstairs.

We drove back to Paris – again there was no conversation between us. He dropped me off at Rue de la Victoire and disappeared.

The next evening at dusk, the time of day when the French say the light is such that you cannot tell if the beast in front of you is a dog or a wolf (*entre le chien ou le loup*), I told Gavin about this episode. He looked worried, which is unlike Gavin because he is usually pretty crazy and up for almost anything. "Listen, Cliff. This guy could be in the Mob. I've heard he's an arm breaker and a bag man. He's probably setting you up to work for him. Watch out. He's got a bad reputation on the street."

Gavin was acting like my big brother, but my curiosity overrode Gavin's warning.

A few weeks later, I came into Le Palmier after a show. It was August. Jean-Paul was sitting alone. He ushered me to sit with him. When a few other dancers approached our table, he told them not to sit with us. It was obvious he wanted to speak with me privately.

He twirled the half-filled red, white and blue ashtray in front of him, and drained his wine glass. Then he popped the question and everything between us up to this point fell into place. I realized that he had been testing me – taking me to private clubs to gauge my temperament and personality. Whether I could keep quiet, and not ask any questions.

"Cleef, can you get diamonds from South Africa?"

He put his hands in his jacket pocket, and as was his habit, fiddled with a set of keys. The expression on his face didn't change, nor did the tone of his voice. He could have been asking me if I thought it was going to rain tomorrow.

I asked, "I presume you want diamonds *smuggled* out of South Africa?"

He nodded. "I have people in Paris who will give you two to three million francs. Then you'll go to South Africa with the money and bring the diamonds back – uncut, of course. Can you do this, Cleef?"

I was way in over my head, but I was willing to play along to see where things might lead. "Well, I know of people who have gotten diamonds out. I know there is a way. I've never done it, of course. I suppose you'd fly charter from Johannesburg to a small airport in Angola or Nigeria where the security is lax. And from there, you'd work your way north, and eventually catch an international flight back to Europe – Paris or London, maybe."

"Right."

"And how large a haul would three million francs buy in uncut diamonds?"

"About a tin cup full. You'd put them in a briefcase and carry them with you at all times. Better than putting them in your luggage, which could be inspected by customs at Heathrow or Charles de Gaulle?

"And what would I get paid if I agreed?"

"Ten percent. You'd make somewhere between three hundred thousand and four hundred thousand francs, depending upon the negotiated price beforehand."

(In dollars that would have been about $80,000 at the time, which was 800,000 rand, enough to buy a palace in Johannesburg or a mansion on the beach in Capetown.) It sounded tempting, and I wasn't morally averse to smuggling diamonds. I would never have agreed to smuggle drugs, but who was I hurting by bringing in diamonds or any other gemstones or precious metals? The term "blood diamonds," had not even been coined at that time, and I was ignorant about the treatment of blacks in the mines or how terrible the conditions were.

Jean-Paul hardly blinked when he said, "You won't know where the money comes from. All this is handled anonymously to protect the 'bank.' And my people are interested in only one thing – diamonds for cash. If you get caught, you are on your own, and they'll want their money back, and they will stop at nothing to get their money. Don't even think about running off with the money. That's not going to happen. They'd kill you first. Do you understand me?"

"What happens if I get stopped at an airport and the

customs officials confiscate the diamonds and put me in jail?"

"They want the diamonds or the money. If they don't get one or the other, you are responsible. Do you understand me?"

"I'm on my own."

"*Exactement.*" He slid his hand down his silk tie and everything went back to normal as if none of this conversation had taken place. He touched me on the shoulder. "Do you want a whiskey?"

My head was spinning. I thought about all the money I could make. Before we parted, Jean-Paul said, "Think about it. You've got to let me know soon."

Chapter 13: In Or Out

Those who meet inside this circle will surely live or die within it.

Jean-Pierre Melville, *The Red Circle* (1970)

The prostitutes working Pigalle were monitored by tough guys riding around on Vespas to blend in with the quotidian traffic. They could have afforded Bentleys or Rolls Royces, but that would have been too obvious. They'd watch the action on the street to make sure that none of their customers took advantage of the girls or beat them up. Some of the patrol looked more like California surfers than mobsters with long, blond hair tied back in a ponytail. One of these lackeys – who were in charge of collecting the cut – had seen me hit Chantal Ortolan. Although Monsieur Clerico assured me that he would take care of everything and that I shouldn't worry, I felt like I was being watched. As I was leaving the Moulin Rouge after the second show, I saw a Vespa pull out from an alley. The guy followed me as I crossed Place Blanche. He looked at me and then sped away.

Jean-Paul was sitting at Le Palmier, his back to the wall. I had not yet given him my answer. He didn't even bring up the diamonds. He said, "I heard what happened to you with that Moroccan prostitute, Chantal Ortolan. They're still on your case. This is not good. We're going to have a sit down."

I thought *How the hell does he know? Did someone tell him? Is he part of the prostitution ring?* Things were getting bizarre. I said, "Who are we having a meeting with?"

"No questions. Just be here after the second show

tomorrow night." Be a good soldier. Take your orders. Yes, sir. No, sir. I was starting to feel hemmed in.

* * * *

I scanned the café. Most of the tables were taken up with the Moulin Rouge Company, and theatergoers who were not ready to take the Métro back to their hotels. They wanted to soak up the atmosphere of Le Palmier and the Place Blanche. Jean-Paul was sitting at a table across from a pony-tailed lackey, who had appeared out of nowhere on his Vespa the evening before. I could feel the tension between them and wondered who was going to pull out a weapon first. I sat down, and the conversation continued in French. All I could understand was "*oui,*" "*non,*" and "*merde alors.*"

"Jean-Paul, I don't understand what you guys are talking about."

"Just sit there and don't say anything. I've got this under control." He waited for a minute as the guy continued to bark at him, and then Jean-Paul said, in perfect English, "If you want a war, we'll give you a war, but Cleef is working for us." My heart started pounding in my chest.

Two thugs were standing behind Jean-Paul, and they moved in closer to protect him. Another matching pair of thugs stood behind his adversary, and I was sitting in the middle of what was obviously a turf war.

With an air of nonchalance, Jean-Paul lit a cigarette and put the lighter back in his pocket. He took a drag on his cigarette and blew the smoke in a long stream. "We know what Cleef did to that *putain*, Chantal. But he's under our protection. If you want to mess him up, you'll have us to deal with. *Compris?*"

Jean-Paul was pushing me into a corner. He was implying, "We'll give you protection if you cooperate with us and get us the diamonds. That's the only reason you are valuable to us. Otherwise, you are on your own. And these guys mean business. They can easily wipe the street with your face."

I wondered if the whole incident with Chantal Ortolan was just a set up to get me to cooperate with Jean-Paul – maybe she had been after me as a ruse so that Jean-Paul could then offer me protection in exchange for smuggling diamonds. I would be in his debt, so to speak. I turned this theory around in my mind. *Had Chantal just been bait? Was she actually working for Jean-Paul?* One thing was clear; I had to make a decision about the diamonds.

You can't put anything past guys like Jean-Paul. They pretend they are your friends, but they're not. It's all about what they want from you. From the first day that Jean-Paul approached me, he was planning to proposition me. Knowing that I was a tough guy, a bit of a vigilante, and from South Africa, I had the right credentials to work for him. He also knew that I could keep my mouth shut. I was too smart to go to the authorities. And if I did, what could I tell them? Nothing. He had made sure of that. I realized that was why he wanted to go to my apartment the night we fooled around with the girls we had picked up. He didn't want me knowing where he lived. It was a simple as that. I couldn't even tell the police where the private club was in the countryside or if his name was really Jean-Paul Caboche.

What I did know for sure was that he could have had me knocked off. He wouldn't have done it himself. He would have hired someone. One evening, coming back from the Moulin Rouge to my apartment on the Rue de la Victoire, a car would have pulled up beside me, and the passenger would have rolled down the window and blown my brains out with a 38, and sped off without a trace. And who knows? The police might have turned a blind eye, not wanting to get involved.

The two men carried on in French for a few more minutes. Jean-Paul turned to me, "Okay we have an understanding. I just saved your ass." Then the blonde haired guy stood up. I stood up, too, taking full advantage of my height. He shook my hand and said, "Cleef, it's finished. It's done. No problem. *D'accord*."

I responded "*Merci*." He walked out of Le Palmier, shoulder to shoulder with his bodyguards. Then Jean-Paul stood. "I have to go. We'll talk again. You need to give me an answer." I watched him climb into his Porsche, and he disappeared into the night.

I ordered a whiskey to calm my nerves. Then I drove to Gavin's apartment. I rang the doorbell downstairs, and he let me in. Sally was fast asleep, but he was awake watching the news on television and drinking straight from a bottle of whiskey.

"What's up man? You look like shit."

I told him what had happened. Gavin played the big brother role, again. "Look, if you do something for Jean-Paul, you might make a lot of money. But that won't be the end of it. You can't just do a one-off. They'll expect you to do it again – if you are successful – and before you know it, the Mob will own you. You won't be able to get out. And then they'll want you to bring drugs into France. It will just escalate." He confirmed what I was already thinking.

And just to put the proverbial icing on the cake, Gavin said, "The French have a saying: *Celui qui se couche avec un chien se lève avec des puces.'* Sleep with a dog and you'll wake up with fleas."

"Man, that's classic."

I realized I had to risk backing out before it was too late. If Jean-Paul took his protection off the table, I could always go back to Monsieur Clerico although I suspected he might already know something about this. But that was sheer speculation on my part. I should probably have stopped reading crime novels and stuck to books about romance.

It was early September. I had known Jean-Paul for two months and was now a principal at the Moulin Rouge. I had plenty of money in my pocket, a beautiful apartment, and lots of girls, both at the Moulin and elsewhere. Sophia was back and forth from Rome. I'd see her for a few days at a time. I was still in touch with my old girlfriend, Liz, who I had left behind in South Africa. We were not on such good terms, but I was thinking about inviting her to Paris sometime after the New Year. I had no earthly reason to accept Jean-Paul's offer except that it was dangerous, and I still had not had my fill of living on the edge. But I saw no point in sticking my head in the crocodile's mouth, as it were. I had a lot of living to do, and I didn't want to end up floating in the Seine River.

I didn't know how Jean-Paul would react, but I told him I couldn't accept his proposal. I said, "It's way too risky. I don't want to dive from a cliff without a safety net to catch me if something goes wrong. And eventually, something will go wrong." I waited for his reaction. He just shrugged his shoulders.

"You sure? I can have the money in your hands in twenty-four hours."

"I'm sure." And then I smiled. "I'd like to make it to twenty-eight. My birthday is tomorrow."

"*Eh bien*. So be it, Cleef. We could have worked well together. But there is always someone else out there. By the way, Happy Birthday."

I never saw him again. After I went back to South Africa, Gavin told me that Jean-Paul had been locked up on some trumped-up charges. The police couldn't prove that he had been running diamonds and other contraband into France, so they charged him with possession of stolen goods. The FBI had also been watching him. He spent a couple years in jail. I never did find out who he really was or where he lived – he operated under the cover of darkness as did the pizza man, and the guys on the Vespas.

I was never approached again by anyone wanting me to get involved in some illegal activity, and there was plenty of that going on in and out of Paris. Nor was I ever harassed by anyone on the street. Jean-Paul or someone else had seen to that. Whenever I walked by, Chantal Ortolan kept her distance, crossing to the other side of the street. Maybe she had become bait for some other ruse. I didn't know, and I didn't care.

Chapter 14: The Clock Is Ticking

Drinking when we are not thirsty and making love year round, Madame: That is all there is to distinguish us from other animals.

Pierre Beaumarchais

By the end of October, the days were getting shorter. The autumn sky turned steel gray as clouds passed over the rooftops of Paris. Often there would be a burst of rainfall, and pedestrians unfortunate enough not to carry an umbrella would run for cover under the awning of the nearest bistro. And then the sun would manage to emerge if only fleetingly before the next shower drenched the city all over again. With the change of season, the Moulin Rouge now presented only one performance a night at nine o'clock which wrapped at eleven, leaving me more free time to test myself physically, have sex, and raise hell with Gavin.

I spent a lot of time backstage at the Moulin Rouge with the company's specialty acts. One night before the show I asked the juggler, Terry, to teach me some of his tricks. His act was amazing. He would sit on a high chair on stage in front of a set of drums and bounce eight balls off the drums. As the beating of the drums sped up into frenzy, the audience went wild. He also used to blow ping pong balls out of his mouth into the air – sometimes moving as many as six or eight balls at the same time. I knew how to juggle at least three balls, but he taught me how to bounce them off the floor. I never did learn how to perform with drums, but I used to juggle in other cabaret acts for years afterward.

The Nicolodi Brothers, Ben, Alex, and Willer, were from a famous family of Italian acrobats. They performed all their tricks in slow motion, which requires a tremendous amount of strength and control. You can't use momentum to carry you through a trick. Their act was set to ethereal music. They would assume these intricate balancing poses à la Cirque du Soleil. For example, Ben would do a one-arm handstand on Willer's head. Ben used to finish their act by doing a series of *flic flacs* across the stage. When he reached stage center, he'd just do them in the same spot. He was literally spinning from his hands to his feet and back to his hands over and over again so that he looked like a sparkling pinwheel. I had never seen anyone do that before. It is extremely difficult. You have to leave the floor and put your hands precisely where your feet are in order to pull the trick off. I made a feeble attempt to copy Ben, but I couldn't do it. It takes many years of training to perfect.

There was a Romanian gymnast in the cast who worked with a trampoline. He used to jump from the trampoline into a handstand onto a bar, and then cantilever himself from a handstand, almost perpendicular to the bar, parallel with the floor. This move requires extraordinary upper-body strength and control and is almost impossible to execute. With all my years as a competitive swimmer, and earlier as a trained gymnast, I still couldn't pull it off. But it was fun to give it a try.

There was a tanning bed backstage at the Moulin. It was there for all of us, and it was free. You always look better on stage with a bit of color, so I used to go in there regularly, as did most of the other dancers. Early one evening before the show, I walked in with only a towel wrapped around me. One of the British girls was already lying on the bed, naked. I asked her, "Do you mind if I share the bed with you?" No one else was around, but if someone had walked in on us, they would have just left, and waited until we were finished. I didn't really know her. She was practically a stranger to me, which made the sex exciting. Afterward, we parted without saying a word to one another. I don't think I ever spent an intimate moment with her again. It was all very amicable, and there were no strings attached. As the song says, we both understood that it was just one of those crazy things.

A few of the gay dancers in the chorus saw me leaving the tanning bed. They joked, "Oh Cleef, you are so naughty. Why don't you share the tanning bed with us?" They knew I wasn't gay, but that didn't stop them from flirting with me. I didn't care, they were great guys.

Nobody in the straight community thought about AIDS. To us, it was a homosexual disease, and promiscuity was rampant between men and women. I remember when I first arrived in Paris and was living on Rue Lepic, I saw a strange encounter. I was walking home from the Moulin. The food stalls on Rue Lepic in front of the cheese shops, boulangeries and small boutiques carrying tourist trinkets were empty of their produce. Earlier in the day they had been filled to the brim with baskets of charentain melons, white and green asparagus, ripe tomatoes, brilliant red and yellow peppers, haricots verts, fish in beds of ice, and red meat hanging from hooks. The intoxicating smells of vine-ripened food still lingered in the nighttime air. As I walked up the street, I heard noises coming from one of the empty vegetable stalls. Two men were having sex in one of the open stalls. A third man was just watching the couple going at it. I wasn't disgusted. I was just amazed that homosexuality was out in the open. Had a gay couple been having sex in a Johannesburg alleyway, they would have been hauled off to jail, taken before a magistrate, and been heavily fined. Homosexuality in South Africa was a crime.

I had a very close gay friend working at one of the other cabarets in Pigalle who was originally from South Africa. He had come to Paris, not only to advance his career as a dancer but to experience the freedom of being an openly gay man. He was very handsome, and had no trouble attracting other gay men, or straight girls, for that matter. Gavin and I used to see him with a different guy every night, and we were worried about him. "Listen, are you wearing protection? If you get AIDS you're going to die." We had already lost a few friends.

He understood. He told us, "I know, I've got to watch it," but he didn't. Somehow he never caught the virus, but one of his South African boyfriends, who he had hooked up with in Paris – died of AIDS some years later.

Billboards started appearing on the streets of Paris sponsored by the health ministry with messages trying to educate the public about the ways that AIDS was transmitted. It was like pissing in the wind; nobody paid any attention, and I never bothered to wear protection when I was having sex. I was just lucky. Five years later, there were over 500,000 reported AIDS cases in the United States alone. I was in Manhattan auditioning for "Guiding Light" for CBS television. It seemed as if every day the *New York Times* carried an obituary of someone who had died of AIDS. I was booked into a hotel near Times Square. I was afraid to use the bathtub or touch the telephone in case someone with AIDS had been in the room before me, and the "germs" might still be lingering.

Casual sex is *normal* in Paris. I had my pick of beautiful girls in the cabarets and elsewhere. Expats, especially those of us from South Africa, where there were strict rules about interracial couples, took advantage of the laissez-faire attitude of the city. In Paris, "anything goes," and sex and love are color-blind.

I met a mixed race girl who was dancing at the Crazy Horse Saloon, an up-market club across from the Georges V Hotel off the Champs-Élysées. She was a dancer from South Africa. Alain Bernardin, the club's owner, and manager considered his six girls part of his harem, and he was very protective of them. Security is tight at the club, and the girls are escorted to their cars by a doorman just in case a patron tries to hit on one of the dancers. Some of the men used to think that the girls were for hire, but that was definitely not the case. They are professional dancers. All the girls perform in the nude and look alike because their pubic hair is painted the same color; they all wear straight black wigs, and they are the same height. They also have the same size breasts, and none of them have implants.

Before the show one evening, a waiter came over to my table at the Crazy Horse and asked me to join Monsieur Bernardin. He had heard that I was interested in one of the girls, Cheryl, and he felt it his duty to protect his investment by interrogating me. "So Cleef, where are you from?"

"Johannesburg."

"And you are dancing at Clerico's place, eh?"

"Yes, sir. I am a principal in the company."

"And before you were in Paris, you were in the military in South Africa?"

I nodded." He had obviously been checking me out before our sit down.

"I hear that you are pretty well known on the street with your friend, Monsieur Gavin Mills, also at the Moulin."

"Yes. He and I are buddies."

He lit a cigarette and through a puff of smoke sized me up. Then he leaned over and patted me on the shoulder. I didn't move. "Okay, I'll let you take Cheryl out. But no funny business. Understood?"

I assured him that she was safe with me and that he had nothing to worry about. I was indulging him – playing with him a bit – because I planned to take her out with or without his permission. Nobody was going to tell me what I could or couldn't do. I was a free man. Besides, Cheryl knew how to take care of herself. In fact, she was too much for me. She turned out to be a nymphomaniac. She wanted sex all the time, nice but exhausting. I couldn't keep up with her, and after a while, I was bored with her. When I stopped seeing her, I swore off sex for an entire month. I needed a break from all that strenuous activity.

Monsieur Bernardin was fighting his own demons. In 1994, he was found shot to death in his Paris office at the age of seventy-eight. The police determined it was a suicide. But who knows for sure? The club had meant everything to him. When interviewed by *Magic Magazine*, two years before his death, he said, "And what we do with the girls is magic, too, because they aren't as beautiful as you see them onstage. It's the magic of lights and costumes. These are my dreams and fascinations that I put onstage."

I understood what he meant. All of us in cabaret were in the business of making magic.

* * * *

Parisians love Christmas. It is an excuse to dress their city up. The display windows at the Galeries Lafayette are famous for their mechanical dolls depicting fairytales and fantasies with mice clanging cymbals, fairies swinging from wires, clocks playing to calliope music. I used to walk by the store on my way to the Moulin Rouge; sometimes I'd go inside and wander from one display case to another – the prices were incredible but so was the merchandise: Chanel, Louis Vuitton, and Dior. It was all there for the price of a small house in Johannesburg. A stained glass dome crowned the interior, which had balconies and gold balustrades on every floor. In the center of the main building was a Christmas tree that reached sixty feet all the way to the dome. Chic women of a certain age – many of them reminding me of my mother – wandered from one department to the next, picking out a present for their husband or for their lover or both.

The pastry shops near my apartment on Rue de la Victoire showed off their *bûches de Noël*, a cake in the shape of a log covered in rich, dark chocolate and stuffed with genoise cream; that was the grand finale of every traditional Christmas family dinner.

Christmas meant nothing to me, but I felt lonely for my family. Neither my father nor my mother had been to Paris to see me perform at the Moulin. This was a great disappointment to me. I felt proud of what I had accomplished. My father's absence – in particular – was in part a sign that he disapproved, once again, of what I was doing. And he probably did not have the wherewithal to buy an airplane ticket. His financial circumstances had taken a down turn according to the letters I received from my mother.

Feeling nostalgic for home, I made a spur of the moment decision to invite Liz to visit me from Johannesburg. I sent her a roundtrip ticket, and she jumped at the chance to see me. The minute I picked her up at Charles de Gaulle Airport, I knew I had made a terrible mistake. I'd been free and easy for eight months in Paris, and all of a sudden I felt restricted by her presence, and couldn't shake the images of our crazy fights during our seven-year relationship. But I couldn't put her back on the airplane right away, and she seemed happy to see me after our long separation.

A friend at the Moulin Rouge had an apartment in Chamonix in the French Alps, and he offered it to me. I took Liz there for a week. We could ski right from our front door under the shadow of Mont Blanc. I had never skied before, but I managed to make it down the trails without disgracing myself. After eight months at the Moulin, I was in the best shape of my life.

Liz and I fell into our old pattern of fighting and making up. Making up under a down comforter with a fire crackling in the fireplace was heaven, but yelling at one another was hell. When we returned to Paris, Liz stayed with me for a few more days at my apartment at Rue de la Victoire. I went back to work at the Moulin Rouge, and she amused herself by visiting the boutiques in my neighborhood. She came to one of my shows. Seeing her in the audience at a table next to the stage made me feel great but didn't make up for my parents' absence.

A few days later, I finished a show, took a shower, got notes from Monsieur Ruggero and Doris, and went over to Le Palmier to have a drink with Gavin and some of the dancers. I was in no particular rush to get back to Liz. At three in the morning, I drove home to Rue de la Victoire. It was still dark outside, but snow had started falling. It was the first time I had seen snow in Paris, and it was magical. The snow softened the outlines of the elegant nineteenth-century buildings, and the snowflakes floated gently through the beams of the street lights.

Liz was already asleep. I fell into bed, not wanting to touch her. We already had our fill of love-making in the mountains, and all I wanted to do was sleep. At eight o'clock, she got up and opened the windows, letting in the morning sunshine, waking me up out of a sound sleep. I yelled at her. "What are you doing?"

"Cliff, we need air in here."

I sat up in bed. I could feel my blood starting to boil. "Didn't you see that I was sleeping? This is my apartment. Don't you dare open the window." I was obviously just looking for an excuse to get rid of her. I just blurted out, "Listen, you've got to go."

"Today?"

"Now." I watched her packing her bag. She stepped into an elegant, turquoise blue dress, pulled her blonde hair into a ponytail, sprayed herself with perfume, and stood at the door with one hand on the doorknob while I pulled on my jeans, a heavy sweater, and leather boots. I grabbed her bag, and we walked into the courtyard. I threw her bag into the back seat of my car, opened the passenger door for her, and got into the driver's seat. As I maneuvered into the morning traffic, I glanced at Liz. She was still beautiful to me, but the petulant expression on her face was a total turn off. I had put it there, but that made no difference to me. I felt some remorse, but I had no intention of apologizing to her for my outburst. I had already spent a lot of my relationship with her apologizing, and I was done.

The snow had disappeared as quickly as it had fallen, evaporated by the heat of the city buildings. I drove Liz to the airport and put her on the airplane. The minute the plane lifted off, I breathed a sigh of relief. I just wanted to be rid of her. I didn't want anything to spoil the euphoria I felt about being in Paris. I realized that I had asked Liz to visit me so that I could decide if I wanted to go back to South Africa to be with her. But after our tumultuous week, I felt in my heart that we had lost our deep connection. Both of us had had other lovers during our separation, which weakened our bond. I knew we couldn't go back to the way things had been, although it wasn't entirely over between us. Old passions sometimes take a long time to die. It usually takes a new love to end an old one. At least, that was true for me.

* * * *

After Liz had bid me a less than fond *adieu,* I felt liberated and ready for another adventure. Joachim, the Swedish principal at the Moulin, approached me backstage in our dressing room. "Cliff, I have a friend who is in Paris for a few days from Stockholm. I think you two should meet. Her name is Asa, and she's gorgeous." Meeting a Swedish girl played into my boyhood fantasies. I had had a serious crush on our Swedish au pair while my family was living in London. I never told her I loved her, but I felt it in my adolescent heart. She was probably three years older than I was, and I doubt she was the slightest bit interested in me. And if she had been, she wouldn't have acted upon it. She didn't want to risk losing her job, and she knew my mother would have gotten rid of her if she detected even a suggestion of mutual attraction. As for my father, he probably would have encouraged me. He always had an eye for beautiful women, especially blondes.

Joachim and I walked across the Place Blanche to Le Palmier. In the café sat a girl in a full – length silver blue, fox coat. She looked like a princess out of a Nordic fairytale with ice blue eyes and shiny long blonde hair. We had an immediate connection. As I remember, she came home with me the first night we met.

Asa's English was perfect, so we had an easy time communicating in and out of bed. She told me that she was in Paris to work with Billy Goodson, who was putting together a show for a corporate client. (He was responsible for the choreography for "Formidable" at the Moulin Rouge so I recognized his name immediately.) She was Billy's assistant and a dancer in the show, and she traveled frequently with him. She stayed in Paris for just three days, but that was long enough for us to make plans to see one another again. I just wanted to be with her. I had put Liz out of my mind, just like that.

Chapter 15: *A Bientôt* Paris. Until We Meet Again

"Allez les enfants, encore une fois. Une autre danse. Peut-être que ce sera ma dernière." (Let's go children, one more time, one more dance. Maybe this is my last.)
Jeanne Avril, *Vedette* of the Moulin Rouge

I was either in, or I was out. My work permit expired in April 1989. I had to make a decision whether to have it renewed so that I could stay at the Moulin Rouge for another year, find work elsewhere, or go home. Asa invited me to work with her on a show in Montreux, Switzerland. I wanted to spend more time with her before I made any final decision about returning to South Africa. I was relieved that I had something and someone to go toward. I wasn't in free fall. I wasn't running away.

I told Thierry, the dance captain, I planned to leave the Moulin at the end of my one-year contract. I couldn't envision another twelve months in "Formidable." The year-round schedule was physically grueling especially during the summer with two shows a night. Plus I had done what I set out to do: I had gone from being a swing dancer to a chorus boy, to a principal at the most famous cabaret theater in the world in less than a year. I had honed my acting technique, and I had been given a speaking part, even if my lines were only "Follow me, my children. Look at Paris." I needed to keep the momentum going, and I was curious about what lay ahead for me. I knew that wherever I went, directors and choreographers would be impressed that I had danced on the stage of this iconic theater. And that has turned out to be true throughout my career.

* * * *

The curtain went up at nine p.m. for my last night's performance in "Formidable." During the show, everyone was knocking into me, kidding around, and trying to make a fool out of me, all in good fun. I took my last look at the sea of faces in the audience: the Japanese tourists sleeping in the front row, the high-class call girls servicing their clients; and Monsieur Henri, Doris, and Ruggero standing in the back of the house with their notepads as they did every night.

For the finale, I changed into my white, three-piece tuxedo, fashioned by Mine Verges, the famous costume house. Debbie de Coudreaux descended the huge staircase, singing "C'est Formidable," dressed in a white-sequined red and white costume as the entire cast paraded around. The women waved their gorgeous feathers, and the men tipped their top hats. The audience broke into wild applause during the finale. Then the master of ceremonies announced the names of each principal for their solo bows. "Monsieur Cleef Simon." That's when I realized that it was over for me. I was sad to be leaving, but the pull to do more was stronger than my desire to spend another year at the Moulin Rouge. A year ago, I wanted more than anything to be accepted into the company, but now I was happy to leave and get on with my life. I had money in my pocket, and visions of an idyllic love affair with my Swedish snow queen in Stockholm filling my mind.

After the show, I visited the girls' dressing rooms for the first and last time. It was usually off-limits. The Mine Verges costumes were still swinging on the racks, just having been removed. The ostrich, pheasant, and cock feathers reminded me of my aviary back in Johannesburg, with all my beautiful birds twittering away. The girls were laughing and chattering as they took off their makeup. Many of them were stark-naked and didn't seem to mind when I walked in. I wanted to say goodbye to the girls I knew – the farewells reminded me of a scene out of "Cabaret," but instead of "*Willkommen, Bienvenue*, Welcome," I heard "*Au Revo*ir, Goodbye and *Auf Wiedersehen*" from the Australian, British, French, Russian, American and German showgirls. I knocked on Debbie de Coudreaux's dressing room door, and when she appeared, I hugged her and told her it was a real honor to have shared the stage of the Moulin with her, which amazes me after we had gotten off to such a bumpy start. I also did the rounds of farewells with Joachim, Thierry, and all the boys. I am happy to say that I am still in contact with Monsieur Thierry to this day. He still sits at the same table, on the first raised section of the theater just to the left of the entrance, with a low light on it so that he can jot down his notes for the cast. The standards of the Moulin Rouge have never waned in all the years, which is why every seat is filled night after night.

I turned in my dance shoes – the Clairvoy label was rubbed off from all the hours I had worn them. I stuffed whatever I kept in the dressing room into my dance bag. I took one last look at myself in the mirror and then walked back out onto the stage. The air was still redolent with the familiar smell of makeup, cigarette smoke, and perspiration. I knew that my spirit would be absorbed into the walls of the theater, intermingling with all the men and women who had performed there before me, and those still to arrive at this great and historic Parisian landmark.

I went back into the boys' dressing room. Gavin was already in his street clothes, and from the look in his eyes, I knew he was up to something. "Sally's out of town, so I am a free man. Want to take one last tour around Paris before we say goodbye?"

It was after midnight, but I didn't feel like going to bed. "Sure, where to?" My post-performance adrenaline was still pumping through my body.

"Let's drive around the Périphérique. We'll go to the Bois de Boulogne. I can't believe I haven't taken you there before. It's Paris at its wildest."

We jumped into Oliver, which was parked outside the Moulin, rolled some hashish and headed for one of the thirty-four ports into the Périphérique. It's a double-ringed road that skirts the circumference of the city. The inside two-lane ring goes clockwise, and the outside ring, counter-clockwise. The speed limit is about forty miles per hour, but at night, there aren't enough police to give out tickets to all the violators. Gavin drove Oliver at break-neck speed. People were hanging out of their car windows, honking their horns, and blaring loud music. If this were a movie, I would have scored the scene with Guns N'Roses' "Welcome to the Jungle."

As we approached the Bois de Boulogne, a caravan of motorcycles slowed down next to us. Most of the riders were transvestites called lady boys. Some of them wore curly blond wigs, leather jumpers with the crotches cut out, and plastic falsies. They'd stand up and wag their muscular behinds in the air inviting drivers to pull off the Périphérique, and take advantage of whatever they had to offer. There were also female prostitutes who dressed in mini-skirts and strappy heels.

Gavin smiled. "Welcome to the world's largest outdoor brothel, Cliff."

I couldn't believe what I was seeing, but after a year in Paris, almost nothing surprised me. That is what I loved about Paris: the freedom, the surprise, the devil-may-care attitude. There were few rules, and whatever rules there were, were intended to be broken if you could get away with it, the opposite of the life I had left behind in Johannesburg. I wasn't sure if I wanted to go back, and if I did, I knew I would always miss Paris and the Moulin Rouge.

Gavin stopped the car by the Bois de Boulogne. During the day, the park is filled with joggers, sports enthusiasts, and horticulturalists. There are numerous greenhouses, several lakes, a sports stadium, and an amusement park. It has the air of Paris during the Belle Époque when the city's residents dressed in their finest and strolled through the green lawns on a Sunday afternoon. By night, the Bois hides all manner of sex acts and all kinds of customers.

There were two gorgeous creatures standing under a streetlight – Gavin, and I didn't know if they were male or female, so we asked them. In answer, they lifted up their tops revealing two sets of gorgeous breasts, but they were very tall, so we still weren't entirely sure of their gender.

Gavin asked them to come home with us, although it can be risky to get involved with working girls. When they heard we were dancers at the Moulin Rouge; they got very excited. One of them said, "Our shift is finished, so we'd like to come with you." Their pimp, who was hovering in the bushes, didn't stop them because they were off duty. We went back to Rue de la Victoire and talked. They spoke some English with thick French accents. We never did discover their gender, because all of us fell asleep with the help of more hashish, and by morning, they had to leave to return to their day jobs as waiters or waitresses. For them, prostitution was a way to earn extra money, have a good time, and a route to something better, although they told us they liked what they were doing on the street.

In later years, the ranks of French and Italian prostitutes were infiltrated by foreigners from all over the world looking for a better life: Brazilians, Indians, Thais, Indonesians, and Filipinos. Some of these expats were outright gangsters, who preyed upon one another. Today, there are numerous reported murders committed in the Bois de Boulogne, which is bad for the tourist trade. The police are trying to clamp down on the perpetrators, but they are too numerous. The trick is to keep them out of Paris in the first place, but the French immigration laws are very liberal. The city couldn't function without foreign workers who are willing to take the jobs that Parisians would consider too demeaning.

Paris never failed to surprise and amaze me and our night with these two working girls – whatever their true gender – was but one more example of the uniqueness of the city I had come to love. I had arrived there under the false illusion that I had a job, and I was leaving having achieved more than I had ever dreamed possible. Looking back on that year, I think I also grew up – leaving home was the best thing I could have done, although I always missed my parents terribly, and the one regret I carried with me was that my parents – especially my father – never bothered to make the effort to see me perform at the Moulin Rouge. But I forgave him; it wasn't in me to hold a grudge against my dad. But I still wanted his approval – I'd just have to wait for that for a few more years, but eventually I was rewarded for my patience. And as for my mother, I knew that I had her unconditional love, and what more could a young man wish for?

Chapter 16: Taking My Blinkers Off

Imagine no possessions
I wonder if you can.
No need for greed or hunger.
A brotherhood of man.
John Lennon, *Imagine*

The blades of the Moulin Rouge windmill didn't stop turning just because I was leaving. The task master, Monsieur Ruggero, found another ambitious performer ready to step into my shoes and subject himself to the grueling cancan training that was Monsieur Ruggero's special brand of torture.

* * * *

On my last day in Paris, I arranged my flight to Stockholm, packed my few belongings, got rid of what I didn't need at Rue de la Victoire, and then at six o'clock – before the evening show – I made one final appearance at Le Palmier.

I ordered a Croque-Madame from the waiter who put on his "cranky" act for the benefit of the tourists around me. He winked as he set my toasted sandwich of ham and cheese with a fried egg down on the zinc tabletop. I ordered a bottle of *vin ordinaire* for Luiz, Gavin and Sally, Joachim and his girlfriend, Sandrine (who would become his wife) and Caroline. Waiting for them to gather, I visited the toilette – a crude drop hole, which must have been an homage to Le Palmier's ancient roots. The toilet was eventually modernized, but there was still only one bathroom for men and women. The customers didn't seem to mind. Le Palmier was not in the business of catering to prissy tourists who might have expected separate toilets for men and women. This was Paris, after all.

I toasted Gavin and thanked him for giving me the key to Paris. Years later, I'd replace him in a cabaret show in Portugal at the Casino Estoril. Luiz stayed in Paris for a few more years, until he couldn't take the rigors of the dance world. He moved to the Algarve in Portugal and opened a hotel for canines. Joachim continued on as a principal at the Moulin for another decade in "Formidable," but moved to a quiet suburb of Paris, where he and Sandrine raised their children. Pigalle was not a place to raise a family, but he made good money as a principal. He and his family now live in Stockholm. Gavin and Bernadett live in SA with their 2 kids. He is an Author and MD/Owner of Sci-Ryder & DFG Events.

The evening was very mellow – no big sendoff – just fond farewells. A light mist softened the April nighttime air. I took Caroline back to my studio apartment on Rue de la Victoire. She was a very beautiful and sweet girl, and I am ashamed to say that I didn't treat her very well. I think she would have liked something more permanent between us, but I couldn't resist the temptation of other women who were available to me without much effort. I was twenty-seven, I thought I was good-looking, and I was definitely adventurous. I didn't want anyone or anything tying me down.

I invited Tommy, a South African expat living in Paris, to spend what was left of the night with us. He brought his girlfriend, Esther, a black girl from the Ivory Coast. She hardly said two words to us, but from the look on her face, I could tell she was madly in love with Tommy and he with her.

Tommy told Caroline and me his story. Five years earlier,

he was living in Johannesburg. When he graduated from high school, he deliberately refused to register for military service as a protest against apartheid. Staying clear of the arm of the law (military service is compulsory at seventeen); he wandered around South Africa playing guitar and surfing. He eventually went to work in a video store and got in an argument with the proprietress who reported Tommy's whereabouts to the military police. He was looking at a six-year sentence in prison for draft evasion. Tommy slipped across the border into Botswana with only a small bag and his guitar before he could be tried and sentenced by the South African Defense Force. He told us, "I put my guitar and surfboard against the wall, and went 'enee meenee mini mo,' and my guitar won.

He said, "I went straight to the British embassy in the capital city of Gaborone. I told an official my story and asked for his help. I needed a ticket to England."

What happened next was unbelievable. Tommy laughed. "The English guy got on the phone. He called the British embassy in Durban and said, 'I've got a white South African sitting in front of me, asking for political asylum.' A few minutes went by, and he hung up the telephone. 'Get out of my office. I don't want to see you again.' He had no intention of helping me and saw me as a traitor."

He continued, "I went straight to the American embassy. They were very nice to me. They offered to send me to the United States, even pay my college tuition. I thought about it and turned them down. What I wanted was to go to France. There was no French embassy in Botswana, but I met a French representative there, and she offered me a plane ticket to Paris and arranged for a work permit. So I ended up here."

Tommy played his guitar in the Paris Métro stations, like so many musicians getting their start, and was able to earn enough money to support himself from what he collected in his tin cup. The he started writing music and had some success.

He took out his guitar and played one of his protest songs about South Africa for us that he had written for his girlfriend, Esther.

His song, "South Africa, What You Gonna Do When the Truth Gets Hold of You?" became my touchstone. I realized that my opinion of South Africa had radically changed since living in Paris (although it was beginning to evolve after I got out of the military). I had dated dark-skinned women, white women, and everything in between. I had seen interracial couples at ease with one another, and no one gave a damn. I could no longer accept the politics of the South African government. I had been like a fish who doesn't know it is swimming around in water until it is thrown onto dry land. But South Africa was still my home. My parents and two of my three sisters lived there. I am proud to have African blood in my veins, but listening to the words of Tommy's song; I knew that if I returned to South Africa, I would have to leave it again someday.

As the night ended, and we finished off what was left in the wine bottles, I fell asleep. I didn't even think about saying goodbye to Caroline in a way that might suggest that she meant anything to me, although we had been together on and off for almost a year. I was such a rebel and admittedly narcissistic at the time. I just kissed her, and that was that. She went back to dancing at the Nouvelle Eve with Luiz. I never tried to reach out to her again.

All I could think about was hopping a plane for Stockholm and wrapping my arms around Asa in her long, blue fox coat and ravishing blue eyes.

Chapter 17: Ice Queen

Switzerland is a country where very few things begin, but many things end.

F. Scott Fitzgerald, *Switzerland and the Swiss*

After a short flight out of Charles de Gaulle airport, I landed in Stockholm. Asa was waiting for me. We went directly to her apartment. She filled a bathtub with hot water and poured in lavender smelling salts. I don't remember anyone ever doing that for me since I was a little boy when my mother used to run me a bath. I felt totally coddled and cared for by Asa. She made me feel right at home. For our first meal together, she put out a crispy flatbread and spread salmon paste over it. I looked out the window. It had started to snow, a heavy, late season snow, unlike the light dusting that falls from the Paris sky. In the morning, the streets glistened with snow, and the temperature was cold enough so that the white blanket did not melt as the day wore on. It was truly magical. I filled my lungs with the icy air, and my stomach with a delicious smorgasbord at a local restaurant near Asa's apartment, where customers downed a serious amount of vodka.

For the next week, we rehearsed the show, which Asa was producing for a corporate client in Montreux, Switzerland. I don't remember the company's name, but it had something to do with housewares and furniture – a precursor to the "Big Box stores" in America like Home Depot. It might have been IKEA, the Swedish retail chain.

In one number, I played the role of a mime and put my juggling skills to good use, which I had learned from Terry at the Moulin Rouge. Asa and I performed a *pas de deux*, and she and I did a mini cancan. I also did some acrobatic moves. The music for the show was written with lyrics about the company, all geared to revving up employee sales and morale.

The studio in Stockholm where we rehearsed was owned by a black South African kung fu master. He told Asa that so long as she was seeing me, he couldn't be friends with her. He said, "I hate this guy. I can't believe that you are actually going out with a white-ass bigot. For god's sake, he fought against the ANC."

When Asa told me what he had said, I was mad as hell. I yelled at her, "Who's being the racist? Him or me? He doesn't know a damn thing about me or my views." It was a real sore point in our relationship.

We temporarily side barred our argument. I didn't want to bring it up again, and I wanted to stay focused on the show. After a week of rehearsals, a group of us flew to Montreux. We stayed in the four-star, Hotel du Grand Lac Excelsior on Lake Geneva at the foot of the Swiss Alps. The hotel was a birthday cake confection of whiteness; each room facing the lake had a spacious balcony with a blue awning. I had never been treated to such luxury before, and I relished every minute of it. We performed the show in a banquet room, which had been reserved by our client, in the fourteenth century Chateau de Chillon on the banks of the lake. During the tourist season, the castle was one of Montreux's main tourist attractions. The salon had medieval murals and tapestries on the wall, and there was a winding stone staircase that led to a parapet perfect for viewing the mist-enshrouded lake. Asa had rented a moveable stage and elaborate lighting. It was a very slick production, and we all made a lot of money. After the show, Asa and I went back to our suite at the hotel. The lobby was a model of Swiss efficiency with attendants dressed in perfectly tailored uniforms, and a concierge in a tuxedo. Again, Asa drew me a bath (this must have been a Swedish custom). We soaked our tired muscles in the hot water and polished off a bottle of Veuve Clicquot.

Asa and I went back to Stockholm and lived together for three months after our performance in Montreux. Her very sweet parents were willing to vouch for me so that I could obtain a Swedish work permit, but I was getting itchy feet. I needed to sort things out in South Africa with Liz. I didn't have the promise of a job there, but I had enough confidence in myself, that I felt I could find work in a cabaret, and eventually, start acting, which would eventually be my stepping stone to the United States, which had become my goal: to end up in Hollywood in the movies.

I left half my clothes in Asa's closet, and my favorite leather boots under her bed with the intention of coming back if she would have me. I felt ambivalent about going home. I still wasn't entirely sure that I wanted to go back to South Africa permanently, or just take one final shot with Liz while keeping the door open to return to Asa and stay in Europe. I didn't say how long I would be away because I really didn't know, and I certainly didn't want to be held to any timetable. I was probably asking a lot of Asa, but at the time, I really didn't give it much thought.

Chapter 18: *Bulle de Bonheur*, **Bubble of Happiness**

I've got you under my skin. I've got you deep in the heart of me.

Cole Porter

I landed at Jan Smuts Airport. It was August – the middle of the South African winter. As I went through customs, I could see my mom waving at me through the glass partition separating the early morning travelers from the waiting crowd. Tears were rolling down her cheeks. In that moment, I realized how much she had missed me, although her letters to me were always cheerful and encouraging. In my heart, I knew that she wanted her only son back in South Africa. I couldn't bear to tell her that I might be home for just a short while.

When I hugged her, I realized how much I had missed her as well, and I became very emotional. I turned away from her and quickly picked up my suitcase hoping that she wouldn't see the tears in my eyes.

I studied her behind the wheel of her car. "Mom, you look great."

"Do I? I'm on another diet. I just can't get myself to exercise."

"Any men in your life? Or is that too personal a question?"

"Just you." She laughed. "I'm not really interested. One husband was enough to last me a lifetime. I've got plenty to keep me busy. I like my job at the *Jewish Times* quite well. I've got my charity work, your sisters, and the grandkids. It's a full life."

I wondered if my mom ever thought about what we all

referred to as "the glamorous days" when she and my father went to swanky parties in Johannesburg and stayed out late into the night.

Mom asked, "And you? Do you have anyone special? What about the Swedish girl?"

"It's complicated. We'll see. I still need to figure out if there is anything left between Liz and me."

"Hmm, your father and I always liked her, but you were too young. You seem to have matured a lot, Cliff. I never thought I would say that, but you have. I am happy for you, darling. The year in Paris has been good for you." I wasn't sure what she was picking up about me in the few minutes we had been together, but I was happy that she saw a change in me – that perhaps I had grown up a lot – that I had an air of self-confidence about me, that wasn't just attached to my looks, that maybe there was something else that made me feel more sure of myself.

It was just a short drive from the airport to my mother's new house. While I was in Europe, she bought a townhouse with a garden full of flowers in a quiet suburb of Johannesburg called Hyde Park. Our old family house in Glenhazel had been torn down. The entire neighborhood was converted into townhouses behind high walls. Where a few large houses had once stood with rolling lawns that blended into one another, there were now fifty families living cheek by jowl. It was a bit sad, but a sign of the changing politics and economy of South Africa.

My sisters Karen and Shelley were waiting for us when we pulled into the driveway. It felt wonderful to be surrounded by their love. Mom made a pot of tea and served us her freshly baked blueberry scones. I relished being fussed over, but after a few days, I moved out of mom's house and rented a small apartment in Johannesburg on a short-term basis.

About two weeks later, I went to see my dad who was living in Durban with his girlfriend. Outwardly, he was not a particularly affectionate man, but I could tell that he was happy to see his rebel son. He always had difficulty showing his emotions, but I accepted that about him and loved him nonetheless. I have been told I hide my feelings too, and I guess that I'm "guilty as charged."

Even in late middle age and in declining health, Dad was always looking for ways to make money. He was selling commercial real estate in Durban. He also had invented a new gadget, a Bike-o-Beacon. It was an orange flag sitting on top of a fiberglass pole, which attaches to your bicycle, and when you are riding in traffic cars can see you. It was a brilliant idea, and he could have made a fortune because it was so cheap to manufacture, but he never got a patent and didn't follow through on his plans to manufacture it – either because he didn't have the money or he didn't fully believe in it. Either way, it was just another in a series of near-successes in my father's life. I always admired his ingenuity but suspected that he must have experienced a lot of disappointment. He never had the benefit of a good education, or family connections to rely upon, like so many successful people he socialized with. In hindsight – it must have been very frustrating for him.

My dad looked very tired and gray. I think the stress of not having a permanent home and the warmth and comfort of a real family, had taken its toll on him.

"Dad, have you been taking care of yourself?"

"Yes, it's all fine. Doctors, eh who needs them."

I then took a deep breath and said what had been on my mind. "Dad, I was disappointed not to see you in Paris."

"Well, travel is expensive these days, and I really didn't know how long you were going to be there. I can never predict what you're going to do with your life."

"I would really have loved you to see me in a professional show like the Moulin Rouge as it might have made you accept that being in the entertainment business is legitimate, and it's my career."

Jokingly, he said, "Well, it still would have been better if you had become a nice Jewish doctor or an attorney. You certainly have the brains for it."

I needed to defend myself, "No to Oxford education, but I have had an education in life, and love what I am doing, that is the most important thing."

Smiling he said, "I'm glad you're happy."

"Dad, I hope I get to see you more often now that I'm back. Stay in touch and don't be a stranger." My father stood up and hugged me. I don't remember the last time he had done that. We didn't see much of one another after that. It was partly my fault – I was traveling a lot for my career, and he was slowing down as his health took a turn for the worse.

After I got back from Europe, I registered with a modeling agency in Johannesburg and moved into the top floor of an enormous mansion where the agency had its offices. It was very posh, and the owner of the agency gave me free rein of the private apartment, which made life very pleasant. She took a serious interest in my career and predicted that I would do well for the agency and for her. In quick order, I was appearing in commercials and music videos. I was putting everything I had learned at the Moulin Rouge to good use, and I started making a lot of money.

I invited Asa to Johannesburg, convinced that I would show her a good time, and we could pick up right where we left off. I didn't ask her to, but I hoped she would pack my leather boots in her suitcase.

She came for a brief visit, but it didn't work out for us. She was uncomfortable with the politics of South Africa. At this time, Mandela was still under house arrest. She didn't like what she saw – some of her best friends in Sweden were black – and she criticized me for even continuing to live in a country that enforced apartheid. I tried to defend myself. "Look I grew up here. I didn't make it like this. And eventually, it's going to change." But she would not be persuaded. She also knew that I wanted to go to the United States someday, and this was not how she saw her life unfolding. After a short time, she told me, "Don't bother coming back to Sweden. You'll just be using me as a stepping stone." And she was right. She knew me better than I knew myself. And there was another factor. I was seeing Liz again. I was trying to keep all my options open. I honestly believed that I was in love with two women, and soon there would be a third girl who completely stole my heart.

After Asa left, I continued performing at various cabarets in Johannesburg. My ex-choreographer Denise Britz, who I had worked with in Durban, invited me to a show and said,

"There is someone I want you to see. She's gorgeous, and she's your type of girl." When Colette stepped onto the stage, I knew immediately that this was the girl Denise was talking about. She was just seventeen. If she had tried to get into the club as a customer, she would have been turned away for being underage, but she was allowed to work there. I went back to the dressing room and invited Colette out for a drink. She refused me. "I have a boyfriend. No, thank you." I found it odd that Denise had encouraged me to meet her. I didn't want to leave the club empty-handed, so I picked up another dancer. Colette saw me leaving the club with her, but I don't think it made an impression on her one way or the other.

A year later, the modeling agency booked me for a commercial for Southern Sun Hotels in Thaba'Nchu, a black free state within South Africa. They had their own police force and special laws allowing gambling, which was prohibited in South Africa proper. The name Thaba'Nchu means "Black Mountain" in Bantu, and the area's major tourist attraction – other than the gambling casinos in the midst of the wilderness – is the Maria Moratia Game reserve, home to the devilishly dangerous white rhino. I didn't like seeing the beauty of the bush marred by a big modern hotel, and tour buses dumping gamblers off from Johannesburg or Pretoria, but a job was a job. I shot the commercial and then went to a show at the hotel. It felt like Kismet – Colette was in the show. I invited all the dancers to come back to my hotel room after the performance. The only girl to knock on my door was Colette. I jumped out of the shower, and wrapped a towel around me, still dripping wet. I must have looked like I only wanted one thing from her, but I didn't intend that at all.

Colette was very beautiful with long curly blonde hair, huge blue eyes and a body to die for. She was very sweet and soft spoken – a real lady – very different from most of the dancers I had known who were party girls. I excused myself, got dressed and ordered tea and before I finished the first cup I tried to hold her hand, but she pulled away. She stood up and said, "I think I better leave." A few minutes later there was a knock at my door. She was standing there. She leaned over and kissed me on the cheek. "Good night, Cliff," and then she disappeared. That was it. I was in love.

I could not get her out of my mind. I went back to Johannesburg and was booked constantly in one music video after another. I finally got up the nerve and called Colette. "Why don't you come to Johannesburg? There's lots of work here. I can plug you into the scene." She was living and dancing in Durban, at the time.

She broke up with her boyfriend whom her parents viewed as eminently appropriate for her and moved to Johannesburg to be with me. I still had the reputation of being a "bad boy" and Colette was warned by a cousin to stay away from me, but, fortunately, she didn't listen. I was still seeing Liz, and I had Asa in the wings back in Stockholm. I was arrogant enough to believe that she would come back to Johannesburg again if I picked up the telephone. I was playing the three women like a poker hand. Eventually, my bluff would be called.

Colette and I were performing together at a show at the Wild Coast Sun Hotel, in an area between Durban and Capetown. About a month or so later, I felt I still hadn't settled things with Liz. I told Colette, "I'm going back to Liz. I have to finish what I started." I drove two hours, and as soon as I walked in the door, and saw some of my clothes still hanging in her closet, I knew I was done. I threw everything into a suitcase, and turned right around and drove back to the Wild Coast Sun, and Colette. She looked at me like I was certifiably nuts. I said the two words that are almost not in my vocabulary, "I'm sorry." She didn't say anything. I kept going, "I'm back. I want to be with you. I don't want to be with Liz. It's done. It's over for good."

"Are you sure?"

"Yes, I'm positive. I have never been more sure of anything in my life."

She looked at me. "No more phone calls to Liz or Asa. It's me or nothing. Can you do that?"

"I promise."

* * * *

By 1991, I had shot eleven television commercials. I was everywhere: on billboards, in print, and on the catwalk. I was getting overexposed and needed to pull back. One day I'd be in a video for a hotel chain riding bareback on a black stallion, and the next strutting the runway in a Hugo Boss suit. The modeling agency was doing too good a job – I became a cash cow for them, and I felt like I needed to take a break, and change the direction of my career. I wanted to back off dancing and modeling and find a way to act full-time with the goal of trying my luck in the United States. I felt that Hollywood was the real test of my talent, but I knew I wasn't ready yet to make such a dramatic move. I didn't have real acting experience.

I entered the first Mr. South Africa competition. The competition was held in a shopping center in Pretoria and was televised on MNET South Africa and covered in society and men's fashion magazines. Mr. South Africa was not a male model, but "a model male" who was expected to be an ambassador for South Africa and an inspiration to young men. One of the prizes for the winner was an audition for a walk-on part in South Africa's first bi-lingual daily soap opera, *Egoli: Place of Gold.* My mother and my two sisters sat in the audience cheering me on during my acrobatics and dance routine. My father was nowhere to be seen. He was in Durban and couldn't be there, which was a disappointment to me, but not unexpected.

I won the Mr. South Africa competition from among twenty entrants and earned an audition with *Egoli,* which was the reason I wanted to try out in the first place. I met with the show's producer, Franz Marx, an Afrikaaner, who had a solid reputation in the entertainment world. A man about town, he was rich, drove fancy sports cars, and was very dapper. I learned that he was half-Jewish. In addition to producing *Egoli*, he directed and produced numerous feature films in South Africa, mainly for the Afrikaans-speaking audience. Even though he could have worked in the United States, he chose to work in South Africa because of his love for the people and the country.

After winning the Mr. South Africa competition, Franz offered me a walk-on part in *Egoli* as advertised. To Franz's surprise, I turned it down. I had something else in mind. "No thank you. I want to study acting and come on the show in a real speaking part." He was impressed with my moxie. Franz saw that I wasn't desperate, and he admired that quality in me. We really clicked. Unbelievably, his entertainment company, Franz Marx Films, offered to pay for private acting lessons with a view to hiring me if I did well. Mila Louw, an acting coach in Johannesburg, agreed to take me on as her pupil, and the plan was that she would inform Franz Marx Films when and *if* she thought I was ready to go on the show. We worked together every day at her studio. At the end of four months, she called Franz and said "Hire Cliff." I went into the show in 1992 as Gregory (Mitch) Mitchell, playing the part of a chief financial officer of a South African company, who was a widower with one child. I was an instant fan favorite, and after just three months, I was offered a contract role and stayed with the show for seven years – the longest run of my career at that point. At thirty-years-old, I hung up my dancing shoes forever, stepping into my acting career, thanks to Franz Marx. This was the opportunity I had been looking for.

My dad was incredulous that I was actually earning a living as an actor no matter how much money I was earning and how celebrated I became. He was happy for my success, but he never stopped teasing me, "When are you going to get a real job, Cliff?" Dad was old school – A Quid Each Day (QED). In spite of himself, he used to brag to his friends about my success and got a great kick out of seeing me on television, and getting compliments about my performance from his friends. I knew at this point that he really did not support me in my career and that only made me try harder and shoot for the moon and the stars beyond. Every son wants their father's approval, and I was no exception.

Of course, I always had my mother's support. She used to call me every day to discuss the previous evening's episode. "Why are you being so nasty to your girlfriend?" or "Just be sure you take care of your little girl now that she's been diagnosed with cancer. How terrible."

"Mom, it's only a television show, but thank you for being my biggest fan."

I got a call from the producers of *Guiding Light*, a CBS television soap opera in the United States. They wanted me to audition for the role of a European prince, and my South African accent worked in my favor. Only two of us had been called in. Franz bought my ticket and told me, "You can make it. You'll pay me back later." Buying my ticket was a way of showing me how much he believed in me. He'd be losing me on *Egoli,* but if I won the part, it would be a feather in his cap. He would win bragging rights that one of his discoveries, Cliff Simon, had broken into American television. I didn't get the part. It went to the blond-haired, blue-eyed American actor, but I was very grateful to Franz for the faith he had placed in me. My trip to New York – my first – gave me a taste of life in the United States, and I knew the minute I stepped into the CBS studios, that I would end up in the United States sooner or later.

I enjoyed the celebrity lifestyle in South Africa. I was always in the glossies. I couldn't go anywhere without someone recognizing me and asking for my autograph. It was a heady time. My girlfriend, Colette, quit the dance world and took a job as a sales rep for a magazine in Johannesburg. My mother adored Colette like a daughter, and after seven years together,

her parents accepted me into the family, and her father gave me permission to marry her, which is what I wanted more than anything else in the world. I had managed to shake off my "bad boy" reputation, at least enough to gain her parents' approval. Colette knew of my dream to come to the United States and was in favor of it. She had never been to the United States, but she believed we could make a go of it together. And she knew that I was finding it harder and harder to tolerate what was happening in South Africa.

Nelson Mandela had become the first democratically elected president of South Africa in 1994. That same year, the government agreed to grant amnesty to persons who fully disclosed their politically motivated crimes of violence. The Truth and Reconciliation Commission gave a pass to people who had thrown bombs and killed innocent people. Among them was Robert McBride (a year younger than me), who had spearheaded the attack in 1986 against the Why Not Restaurant and Magoo's Bar in Durban, which killed three white women and injured sixty-nine people. I was within a few hundred meters of the bar when the bomb went off. Any closer and I would have been blown to smithereens. He was later appointed chief of metropolitan police for Ekurhuleni Metropolitan Municipality. He was just one of many officials with blood on his hands, who was appointed to a position of authority by the ANC in the 1990s. I couldn't believe that those who had committed violent acts against innocent people were not only granted amnesty but were put into positions of power.

What also riled me was the de Klerk government's treatment of 32 Battalion before Nelson Mandela became president. 32 Battalion was the most feared fighting unit of the South African Special Forces. Made up of black, foot soldiers and white officers, it was the *only* desegregated fighting unit of the military, and one of its most decorated. It was also one of the most feared. Its nickname was The Terrible Ones or the Buffalo Battalion. The blacks in the unit were Portuguese-speaking Angolans who had chosen to cross over into South Africa and fight against the insurgents. When the Battalion was disbanded in 1993, the black soldiers could not return to their native countries of Angola and Namibia where they were seen as traitors. In effect, they became a lost tribe. Despite everything they had sacrificed, they were despised by South African blacks for fighting alongside the whites, and shunned by the whites (who had no more say once the government was controlled by the ANC). Most of them were sent to Pomfret, a desert town, formerly the site of an old asbestos mine, to live out their days. I, along with other young people in South Africa who knew about them, was ashamed of the way they were treated in the end.

Life in Johannesburg had become increasingly dangerous as the economic conditions deteriorated. One night when I was on set filming an episode of *Egoli* the director signaled to me that I had an urgent phone call. It was Colette sounding hysterical. Three black guys had come walking into our townhouse in Lonehill through an open patio garden door after tying up the security guard at the front gate of our complex. My two British bull terriers were surprised by the intruders but did not attack them. Harley (the male terrier) started growling, and one of the intruders hit him with a wire coat hanger, which he then used to tie Colette's hands behind her back. They screamed, "Where are the guns and money?"

Colette answered, "Just take whatever you want and leave."

Two of the men ransacked our townhouse while the third threw a duvet cover over Colette's head threatening "Now I am going to kill you."

Colette repeatedly shook the cover off telling him, "If you are going to shoot me, I want to look in your eyes when you do it." His comrades called him to help take stuff over the wall. Colette made a split second decision; her adrenaline kicked into high gear, and she bolted out the front door not knowing if they were about to return. She ran for her life to a neighbor's house. During the break in, she managed to stay in control of herself, and she was unbelievably courageous knowing that at any moment they might have pulled the trigger on the gun that they held to her head.

I flew out of the studio without telling the director what had happened or where I was going. I drove at breakneck speed on automatic pilot not knowing if Colette was injured. When I got home, the police were already there, investigating the situation. I walked in and went crazy. Colette was shaking uncontrollably, but other than bruises on her wrists, she was unharmed. My dogs had run out with Colette and were fine. I was literally ready to kill.

I told the police that I wanted to go with them on patrol, and if we found the cowards, I wanted them to let me into the jail cell with a baseball bat. Without hesitating, they said, "Of course." I got my 12 shot revolving barrel Protecta shotgun and my 38 Special, and we took off for a squatters' camp near our complex. A frightening place. Driving in with the police I felt like I had a target on my back. We eventually spotted 3 guys that fitted Colette's description. After a pretty violent struggle and takedown they were arrested. The following morning Colette hesitantly went to the police station for a lineup, but she couldn't identify any of them with absolute certainty. I was humbled by her bravery and for remaining so calm and clear-headed. She was my hero.

These incidences became increasingly frequent throughout Johannesburg as the economic plight of the blacks in the city became more desperate. Colette and I believed that the next time we might not be so fortunate, and I was tired of playing vigilante. I had my fill of it in Johannesburg and on the streets of Paris. But we were not ready to leave.

We weren't going to run away. When we leave, it will be a positive choice and a belief that we'd be pursuing bigger goals, not escaping recurring nightmares.

Chapter 19: Honeymoon in the City of Lights

Paris is always a good idea.
Audrey Hepburn, *Sabrina*

Colette and I were married on November 1, 1997. I was thirty-five, and Colette was twenty-seven. I never thought I was the marrying kind, but after eight years together, it just felt right to both of us.

Sarie, an upscale Afrikaans magazine, wanted to carry photographs of our wedding. In exchange for the exclusive rights, the magazine paid for the entire cost of our wedding and the after party, which were much more lavish than anything we could have afforded on our own. I certainly didn't do it for the publicity because I was already on South African television every day as Mitch in *Egoli*.

The ceremony was held at sunset near the hippo pool at the Bakubung Bush Game Lodge in Pilansburg National Park, about a two-hour drive into the bush from Johannesburg. The name of the lodge means "People of the Hippo" in Tswana for good reason. Game rangers with rifles had to be stationed at the foot of the hill to make sure that the hippos did not charge any of the guests at the wedding. An angry hippo is a sight to behold. You don't want to find yourself in its path. Those stubby legs can cover a lot of ground quickly, and its mouth can devour a man just like a tasty morsel. Hippos are responsible for more human deaths than any other animal in South Africa.

Fortunately, we had no beastly interruptions from any of the Big Five, who made their home in the park, during the wedding. As the sun dropped behind the Pilanesberg Mountains, the bush came alive with the sounds of wildlife. Porters lit torches, and music accompanied our vows. I was wearing a designer black suit, and Colette was in a white designer gown made just for her. She looked like a fairy princess. A live band accompanied Colette down the aisle. There were lots of flashing light bulbs, and a camera crew recorded the evening for replay on television. All our good friends and the entire cast of *Egoli* were there. After the ceremony, the party was shuttled in mini-buses into the Reserve to a huge *boma,* an enclosure made out of wooden pickets, for dinner. Once you're inside the Reserve, the gates are closed for protection, and you can't get out. Elephants and lions were calling to one another in the bush. There was no electricity; everything was lit with torches and bonfires. The dance band ran their power from a generator. Attention had been paid to the smallest detail by *Sarie Magazine* and Bakubang Lodge.

My mother and my father were seated at separate tables during the dinner hour to avoid any awkwardness. (My father had brought his girlfriend with him.) I'm not sure how my parents felt about seeing one another. Even when love dies, there is always a residue of pain and regret underneath the anger – at least that is what I believe. Colette's parents, her sister, brother and cousins, my sisters Karen and Shelley and their husbands were all there, but my youngest sister Terry was in Israel. She had babies to take care of.

The caterers prepared lamb on spits over huge open pits, and we had every imaginable traditional South African dish. It was very informal but lavish. Waiters passed flutes of Veuve Clicquot, and at the appropriate time, my two best men,

Johnny Leeb, who was a schoolmate, and David Rees, an actor working on *Egoli* with me, delivered the toasts. I got on the stage and sang "Wild Thing" to Colette while she stood on the dance floor. My voice had not improved one bit. I couldn't remember the lyrics. I jumped off the stage half way through the song and told the band to carry on without me.

We danced to "I Swear" by the group All 4 One as our first dance in the moonlight.

When the party was over at one a.m., Colette and I stayed for a few days at the Tshukudu Lodge, which was an exclusive lodge with just ten chalets, run by a woman who maintained a preservation center on the property for wounded and orphaned animals. She was thrilled to have us as her guests and made sure that we enjoyed our private time away from the cameras. She invited us back there for free for our first anniversary with as many friends as could be accommodated.

Colette and I went to the Swiss Alps on our honeymoon. After spending a week or so there, I took her to Paris. The weather was cold and windy for November; there was at least one rain shower a day – so different from the dry, summer weather of the Southern Hemisphere we had just left. I hoped that we might have a light snowfall. The city is even more beautiful with a light coat of white powder on its gray stone buildings.

We walked to my old studio apartment on Rue Lepic, past the Hotel Bellevue, a flea-bag hotel that rented rooms by the hour, with a bar called the Café Moulin as an homage to the windmills, which once-upon-a-time dotted the hillside of Montmartre. In the nineteenth century, there were at least thirty windmills grinding grain for bread, and local vineyards, which bottled and sold wine. Now there were only two or three windmills standing in the eighteenth arrondissement.

We wandered along the narrow, cobblestone streets to the Allée des Brouillards (the Alley of the Mists) and lingered at the Chateau de Brouillards, an eighteenth-century stone house, which fell into disrepair and became the encampment of starving artists until it was bought by an industrialist and restored to its original beauty. Nearby old men were engaged in a lively tournament of *pétanque.* An organ grinder played a lively tune "Frou Frou," which I recognized as the opening song of Jean Renoir's *Grand Illusion.*

From there we climbed up the Butte to Sacré-Coeur. The carousel was still running. Colette climbed onto a white steed, and I took photographs of her. She was wearing a white sweater and jeans and a black scarf, her blond hair tied up in a ponytail.

We walked back down the hill to the Rue de la Victoire. I showed her the courtyard of my apartment at Number 82, and then we stopped at the lingerie store around the corner and looked in the window.

When I performed at the Moulin, I didn't have any real desire to visit the city's tourist attractions. I wanted to feel like a native, and so I skipped going to the top of the Eiffel Tower. Now was my chance. It was a windy day; the temperature had dropped below freezing. When I suggested that we go all the way to the top, Colette hesitated. She is afraid of heights, but I persisted. We got into the huge metal see-through elevator. It was packed with tourists. A South African family stood next to us, jabbering away. The mother kept glancing at me. Suddenly she burst out, "I know you. You're Mitch on *Egoli* aren't you?"

I tried to act as humble as possible, but inside I was bursting with pride. Being recognized in Johannesburg was a daily occurrence for me, but in Paris, that was truly amazing. Colette squeezed my hand.

We changed elevators at the second floor for the ascent to the top, some 1,000 feet above ground. As the doors opened, the wind was howling. I tightened the scarf around my neck and leaned out into the wind. I couldn't see the city below. It was shrouded in a heavy fog, and the rain was coming down hard. Colette stayed back. "Come on," I yelled. She crawled out on her hands and knees but refused to stand up. When the elevator returned, I helped her up, and we jumped back into the car. There was no one else in the elevator. I put my hands on her cold and wet cheeks and kissed her. I whispered in her ear, "We did it. I knew you could." As the elevator descended, I felt like I had come home; Paris was under my skin, and having Colette by my side, made it perfect.

Later that afternoon the rain stopped. Colette and I wandered past the Hotel Georges V and stopped at a café across the street near the Crazy Horse Saloon. We sat down at a small table by the window. I got up to go to the men's room. Passing by the bar, I heard the bartender yell out, "Monsieur Cleef." I turned around and recognized him. He had been the bartender at Le Palmier. We hugged and then chatted for a few minutes. He was very friendly, so unlike the stereotype of what the rest of the world thinks of the French. Once you show them respect, they have a way of greeting you and treating you with genuine warmth. When I got back to our table, Colette poured me a glass of Champagne which nestled in the ice bucket beside us. I said, "It's been eight years since I left, and the guy still remembers my name."

At nightfall, we headed for the Place Blanche. I stood over the Métro grating and felt the heat rising one more time from the underground, and then we went backstage at the Moulin Rouge. Everyone was still there –Thierry, Monsieur Ruggero, Monsieur Henri, Doris Haug, Joachim, Debbie de Coudreaux, Alex, Willer and Ben and backstage crew (I presume Monsieur Clerico was sequestered in his office, watching the proceedings over closed-circuit television)

Colette and I were given seats up front for the show. The Moulin was jam-packed with tourists. Waiters scurried about delivering drink orders before the lights went down and the showgirls appeared on stage. Nothing has changed except that now – instead of being part of "Formidable" – I was feeling very proud sitting in the audience with my beautiful wife. A sense of euphoria washed over me as I watched what I love to do connect with the one I love. Being a trained ballet dancer, Colette was in awe of this iconic venue. She hugged me hard and I melted back into her arms, feeling her breath on my neck. Of course I was waiting to see if anyone on the stage flicked a note at her. If they had, as a joke I would have gone to meet them at the stage door because I knew where it was. Colette and I drank a toast to one another, and to what lay ahead for us. *Merci* Paris, for the most unforgettable year of my life.

<u>The Formidable Program</u>
<u>(1988 – 1998)</u>

Les Doriss Girls

Les Touristes

Formidable

Paris en Rose

À Paris, Les Femmes Ressemblent à des fleurs

Au Soleil du désert

Le Marche

Les Filles aux serpents

Night Club

Les Tapis Volants

La Fontaine Lumineuse

Sur le Prater

Le Dortoir

Les Rockers de Vienne

Allons à l'Opéra

Valses de Vienne

Cancan

La Dance Nouvelle Jeanne Avril/Bruant

Une Pensée pour Maurice

Un Clin d'ceil à Joséphine et Mistinguett

Grand Finale: Blanc et Rouge: Formidable

Acknowledgments

This book would not have been written without the love, support and encouragement of my wife Colette who was my most perceptive reader.

I want to thank my sisters Terry and Shelley and my dear departed mom, Phyllis Simon, my dad Emanuel (Mannie) Simon, and my sister Karen (May they rest in peace). And to my Aunt Barbara Silberman - Cohen, thank you for always taking care of me in my younger years.

Gavin, Joachim, Luiz. My brothers and friends for life. Gratitude all around to Shani – live free my brother – and to my best men at my wedding, lifelong friend, Jonny Leeb, and co-actor David Rees.

Thanks to the Moulin Rouge especially Madame Jacqueline, Monsieur Thierry, Monsieur Ruggero (RIP), Doris Haug (RIP), Monsieur Henri (RIP), Janet Pharaoh, Jacki Clerico (RIP), whose vision for the Moulin Rouge kept every seat filled and his son Jean-Jacques for keeping the torch burning.

And in no particular order, appreciation to *vedette* Debbie de Coudreaux, my friend Pascal (RIP), the Nicolodi acrobats, Terry Parhade, the juggler, and MacBeth, a magnificent scene-stealer on four legs. Karah and Marianne Khavak and Marc Métral.

Thank you to impresario Franz Marx and the entire cast and crew of *Egoli: Place of Gold, (1992-2000)*.

And to Jean-Paul Caboche, Corporal Maclean, Neil McKay (RIP), Denise Britz, Asa, Liz, Andrea, Tommy,

Caroline, Rick Bailey, who could have made me an Olympic swimming Gold medalist if I had co-operated.

Thanks to Barbara Terry at Waldorf Publishing for believing that I had a unique story to tell. Huge thanks to French editor Steve Krief for your invaluable input. Finally, a personal thank you to Loren, my writing partner, for your collaboration, eye for detail and passion. Your love and knowledge of Paris made this book a reality for me.

Some names have been changed to protect the not-so-innocent.

About the Authors
Cliff Simon

A television and film actor for over twenty years, **Cliff Simon** was born in Johannesburg, South Africa to a middle/upper-class Jewish family. At the age of fifteen, he along with his family immigrated to England when the political situation in South Africa threatened his father's livelihood. With a strong, competitive background in swimming and gymnastics, Cliff joined the British swim team, training and ultimately qualifying to compete in the 1984 Olympics. Just short of reaching his goals, he decided to return to South Africa where he enlisted in the Air Force. After surviving two years in the military, he headed for the gorgeous Natal Coast where he spent his days teaching water sports and living the good life. By chance, he was recruited for a nightclub dance show as an acrobat and realized that performing and being on stage was where he wanted to be. He spent many years taking dance classes and performing at entertainment venues throughout South Africa and internationally and appearing on television. His experience as a dancer and performer landed him a spot in the cast of "Formidable" at the iconic Moulin Rouge in Paris, where he quickly rose to the position of principal. When he returned to South Africa a year later, he was snapped up by a modeling agency and was booked for runway and print while continuing to perform in cabaret. He competed in the Mr. South Africa contest and won. The prize included an audition on the first bi-lingual soap opera, *Egoli: Place of Gold*. The show's producer recognized Cliff's talent and charisma, so he sent him for acting lessons, and then offered him a contract role. He spent seven years on *Egoli* where he made a name for himself and generated an impressive fan base. He married his long-time girlfriend, Colette Channell. Wanting to create a better life and setting his sights on greater opportunities, the couple moved to Los Angeles in 2000. He landed a five-year recurring role as the villain, Ba'al in the TV Sci-Fi thriller, *Stargate SG1*, and the DVD movie, *Stargate Continuum*.

Now a U.S. citizen, he's guest starred in many films episodic television shows ,amongst others, all three of the NCIS franchise, *24*, *The Americans, Castle*, and *Criminal Minds: Beyond Borders*. Cliff has 2 film projects coming up in 2018. He's latest film *Project Eden Vol 1* has a USA theatrical release in 2018. Cliff was nominated in 2015 as best guest star for his role on *Castle* by BOTVA in Canada, of course, most of the time playing the villain. Cliff has over 200,000 Twitter followers, which he uses to inform his fans about his career and writing. Cliff spends his down time kiteboarding and paddle surfing from the beaches off Venice to Malibu or relaxing among the palm trees in his backyard with his mix boxer-pit bull, Duma at his side. You can visit Cliff on IMDB, Twitter@cliffmsimon, and Facebook.

Loren Stephens

Steeped in the frantic rhythm of *Jacques Brel Is Alive and Well and Living in Paris*, and the over-the-top comedy of *La Plume de Ma Tante,* **Loren Stephens** jumped at the chance to collaborate with Cliff Simon on this memoir, bringing together her knowledge of theater and film, and her love for all things French. In high school she studied French and traveled to France with a group of American teenagers, staying in tents on the Riviera, living with a family in Grenoble, and marching in a Bastille Day parade in Paris while eating a bag of cacachuètes, oily peanuts from North Africa. Years later she witnessed the May Student uprising in the Quartier Latin, as the pavement was torn up in protest against tuition increases at the public universities. In 2004 she revisited Paris and floated by barge down the Yonne River from Auxerre, managing to get lost in the Burgundy countryside.

Professionally, Loren is president of Write Wisdom, based in Los Angeles where she pens memoirs for her famous and not-so-famous clients. She was previously a film and theater producer. Her credits include the Emmy-nominated *Legacy of the Hollywood Blacklist*, and the bi-lingual *Los Pastores: A Shepherd's Play*, and the Los Angeles stage productions of *The Normal Heart, Loot,* and *To Gillian on Her 37th Birthday*.

Her short stories and essays have been published in literary journals and newspapers throughout the United States and Canada including the Los Angeles Times, the Chicago Tribune, Peregrine, MacGuffin, Sun Magazine and Eclectica as well as the anthologies *Kicking in the Wall* (named one of the best books on the craft of writing for 2014*)* and *Thanksgiving Tales*.

Loren was nominated for the 2015 Pushcart Prize for her short story "The Sushi Maker's Daughter," which is also the title of her just completed debut novel based on her Japanese husband's family saga. You can visit Loren at her website www.writewisdom.com.